Witnesses to a Great Miracle

Witnesses to a Great Miracle

A. M. Deigloriam

RESOURCE *Publications* · Eugene, Oregon

WITNESSES TO A GREAT MIRACLE

Copyright © 2017 A. M. Deigloriam. All rights reserved. Except for brief quotations in critical publications or reviews, no part of this book may be reproduced in any manner without prior written permission from the publisher. Write: Permissions, Wipf and Stock Publishers, 199 W. 8th Ave., Suite 3, Eugene, OR 97401.

Resource Publications
An Imprint of Wipf and Stock Publishers
199 W. 8th Ave., Suite 3
Eugene, OR 97401

www.wipfandstock.com

PAPERBACK ISBN: 978-1-5326-3331-7
HARDCOVER ISBN: 978-1-5326-3333-1
EBOOK ISBN: 978-1-5326-3332-4

Manufactured in the U.S.A.   JULY 17, 2017

Dedicated to my loving wife of 45 years, my family,
and my many friends.

Contents

Introduction | ix

Chapter 1.   God's Plan for Moses | 1
Chapter 2.   Moses and the Israelites Journey | 11
Chapter 3.   Moses Experienced God's Wrath | 17
Chapter 4.   Elijah | 21
Chapter 5.   Peter the Apostle | 31
Chapter 6.   James (the Greater) the Apostle | 46
Chapter 7.   John the Apostle | 49
Chapter 8.   The Transfiguration of Jesus | 59
Chapter 9.   The Transfiguration | 78
Chapter 10.   Application | 93
Chapter 11.   Conclusion | 127

Notes | 137

Introduction

GOD'S LOVE FOR MAN has been revealed and unfolded throughout history by many events. Man has been richly blessed for hundreds of years as God our Father has patiently and lovingly instructed man how to live a holy life. His love for man knows no bounds and His patience seems to be without end. God selected the Apostles Peter, James, and John to see and experience His deity that their lives and ministry may be a complete and a powerful force in building the church and saving millions of souls.

This book acts a reminder that we need to learn from history and alert to the changes in the moral and ethical standards in our culture. Since the fall of man, Satan and his demons have focused on man's weaknesses. They have caused man to struggle with his value of self and ego. The fall of man and the resulting separation from his Creator caused a huge void in man's life. Since that time man has been trying to fill that void with possessions, achievements, and other ways to satisfy his ego and other selfish needs.

Over the centuries kings and queens have tried to dictate who and what people should worship. Moses, Elijah, and the Apostles all struggled with people that insisted they needed to worship pagan gods. The pagan gods of pleasure and self are still present today as people are consumed by spending all of their time and money trying to satisfy their need to find peace and a sense of fulfillment. Our culture dictates that to achieve pleasure and fulfillment one needs to be consumed by materialism.

God's plan for all of mankind was unfolded by a number of events and saints. Moses, Elijah, and the Apostles James, Peter, John all spoke of idolatry and the need to admit it exists and take action to eliminate it in our

Introduction

daily lives. Our purpose, self-esteem, joy, sense of fulfillment, and pleasure are all directly related to our relationship with our Lord and Savior.

The Transfiguration of Jesus Christ was witnessed by Moses, Elijah, James, John, and Peter. God choose these specific saints to be part of this miraculous event due to their status within a group of chosen individuals. Naturally, all of these individuals were considered to be responsible for making major contributions to God's ministry in many different ways and were held in great esteem.

God spoke directly to Moses and told him he and his brother Aaron would need to approach Pharaoh to ask for the release of the Israelites. God spoke directly to Moses ten times giving him and Aaron directions as to how the ten plagues would unfold and how they would impact Pharaoh and the people of Egypt. Moses was about 80 years of age and Aaron was about 83 during this time. Moses died at the age of 120 and Aaron at 123 after wandering for 40 years in the desert. During these 40 years God spoke directly to Moses as a friend and gave Moses instruction as how to direct and lead the Israelites during this difficult journey.

Elijah is considered the eminent prophet mentioned more than any other prophet and was chosen to appear with Jesus at the Transfiguration. God spoke directly to Elijah a prophet of God giving him direction as to where to perform miracles, where to live, and when to move throughout the land of Israel. God worked through Elijah in discrediting Baal as a god to be worshiped by the Israelites.

James the son of Zebedee and the brother of John the Apostle was also chosen to be present at the Transfiguration of Jesus. It is believed due to James' great love for Jesus and his fearless zeal for the gospel that he was the first apostle to be martyred. He was killed with a sword by King Herod's command about 44 AD during the general persecution of the church.

John the Apostle (the beloved disciple) was also extremely close to Jesus and was present with Him during the Transfiguration and during many of His miracles. It is generally agreed that the Apostle John wrote the Gospel of John, the three Epistles of John, and Revelations. Like Peter, John was loved and blessed in many ways.

Peter was the rock that Jesus built His church on, loved by Jesus, and was often by Jesus' side throughout His ministry. Peter left his occupation as a fisherman and became a follower of Jesus. This decision would result in changing Peter from a man that spent his day fishing to a man that spent his day assisting his Savior in presenting the gospel of salvation. It is generally believed that he worked closely with John Mark in writing the book of Mark. It is also believed that he wrote First and Second Peter. No person would predict that a common fisherman would be transformed into one of God's greatest servants.

1.

God's Plan for Moses

GOD'S TIMING AND HOW He plans out events is difficult for us to understand. In many cases His timing and plans unfold over periods of time we cannot comprehend. In some cases we see His plan unfold within a life time and in others cases His plans are fulfilled over many life times. God chose Moses as His messenger and the leader for the Israelites.

Moses' (1393 to 1273 BCE) life was filled with God's presence and direction. Moses is believed to be the author of the first five books (Genesis, Exodus, Leviticus, Numbers, and Deuteronomy) of the Old Testament. There are those who said Moses spoke with God's voice and at the same time was the most humble man to walk on the face of the earth.

Moses' life was a miracle in many ways. He was born at a time when the Pharaoh set a decree that all male Hebrew babies should be drowned. The Pharaoh wanted to control the number of Hebrew slaves for fear He may lose control.

Moses' survival through his childhood was also a great miracle. He was placed in a basket in the Nile River where he was discovered and raised by the Pharaoh's daughter. He was raised within the Pharaoh's household with the best of care and education. At this point, you can see how God is grooming Moses to be the Israelites' leader. At age 40 (Acts 7:23–24), he became enraged one day after watching a guard beat a Hebrew slave and killed the guard. He then fled the country for his life. He later married Zipporah and had two sons (Gershom and Eliszer) after becoming a shepherd in the land of Midian which is located southeast of the Sinai Peninsula.

It wasn't until Moses was 80 years old that God revealed himself in a burning bush at Mount Horeb in the Sinai and instructed him to liberate the Israelites from the enslavement of the Pharaoh of Egypt. God's plan and timing of these events was made possible with men who were able to recognize God's presence and who were obedient to God's word and direction. Moses spirit at this point in time was a willingness to serve (Here I am God use me) without knowing the task at hand.

Exodus 3:4 reads, "And when the Lord saw he turned aside to see, God called unto him out of the midst of the bush, and said, Moses, Moses. And he said, Here am I."

Exodus 3:7 reads, "And the Lord said, I have surely seen the affliction of my people which are in Egypt, and have heard their cry by reason of their taskmaster; for I know their sorrows."

Exodus 3:10-11, "Come now therefore, and I will send thee unto Pharaoh, that thou mayest bring forth my people the children of Israel out of Egypt. And Moses said unto God, Who am I, that I should go unto Pharaoh, and that I should bring forth the children of Israel out of Egypt."

Moses had not been in Egypt for 40 years and many of the people that knew him were dead including the King that wanted to kill him. At this point, he begins to question God's plan for him to return to Egypt and bring the Hebrew people out of slavery from the current Pharaoh. Questioning or asking the Pharaoh to entertain such a request would be in most cases a death sentence. God answered Moses with a clear message.

Exodus 3:14-15 reads, "And God said unto Moses, I AM THAT I AM: and he said, Thus shalt thou say unto the children of Israel. I AM hath sent me unto you. And God said moreover unto Moses, Thus shalt thou say unto the children of Israel, The Lord God of your fathers, the God of Abraham, the God of Isaac, and the God of Jacob, hath sent me unto you: this is my name for ever, and this is my memorial unto all generations."

Exodus 4:10 reads, "And Moses said unto the Lord, O my Lord, I am not eloquent, neither heretofore, nor since thou has spoken unto thy servant: but I am slow of speech, and of a slow tongue. And the Lord said unto him, Who hath made man's mouth? Or who maketh the dumb, or deaf, or the seeing, or the blind? Have not I the Lord?"

God responds to Moses' fears by sending Aaron his brother to be his spokesman and companion as they together journey to Egypt to confront the Pharaoh.

God wanted to remind both Moses and the Israelites of His promise He would be with them always and throughout all their struggles. He is God and all things are possible through Him. Moses certainly was a man of great courage not only to question God, but to obey His command to return to Egypt to confront the Pharaoh. Over and over we see God pick men that seem outwardly not to be men of great leadership skills. We know that Moses was a man that was slow of speech, had a violent temper that led to the killing of an Egyptian guard, spent 40 years as a shepherd, and questioned God's command to go to Egypt. These are not traits one would associate with being a candidate for taking on great responsibility and a leadership role. However, God looks at a man's heart to determine who He will use to further His kingdom. He is able to determine at what point in time a man or woman is ready to share a personal relationship with their creator. As Moses, this relationship begins when a person surrenders to God and grows in dependence on Him for direction.

Exodus 7:1–2 reads, "And the Lord said unto Moses, See, I have made thee a god to Pharaoh: and Aaron thy brother shall be thy prophet. Thou shalt speak all that I command thee: and Aaron thy brother shall speak unto Pharaoh, that he send the children of Israel out of his land."

Moses and Aaron did as God asked and confront Pharaoh with the demand that he release the Israelites knowing they may be killed on the spot. The number of Israelites captive in Egypt is estimate to be 600 thousand not including woman and children. This was a slave workforce that represented great wealth and importance to the Pharaoh and Egypt. The question of release was probably considered ridiculous and its requesters as men of not sound mind.

God's plan was more complicated than just the release of the Israelites. His plan was to bring Pharaoh and Egypt to their knees to realize He was God and no other gods would be tolerated. He would destroy Pharaoh, his army, and create 10 plagues that would destroy the country. God would also harden the heart of Pharaoh so that he would be solely responsible for Egypt's destruction.

THE FIRST PLAGUE

Exodus 7:17 reads, "Thus saith the Lord, In this thou shalt know that I am the Lord: behold, I will smite with the rod that is in mine hand upon the waters which are in the river, and they shall be turned to blood."

All the fish in the river died and rotted in the rivers. There was no drinking water since all the water from the Nile and all other sources were now contaminated and not drinkable. The pagan god of the Nile was no longer a god that would bring forth nourishment to the Egyptians.

Moses and Aaron were persistent in the face of great danger and continued to ask Pharaoh for the release of the Israelites. Moses showed great courage and refused to compromise on his demand and continued to say, "Thus saith the Lord God of the Hebrews . . . let my people go, that they serve me".

The Pharaoh was both the religious leader and the political leader. Their religion was a complex system of polytheistic beliefs and rituals centered on many different pagan deities. Pharaoh was also believed to be a god and the god's representative on earth. His chief responsibility was to maintain peace and harmony throughout the country. He achieved that by working with the pagan goddess Ma'at. He fought battles to protect the country and to gain resources. It is believed that Thutmoses III (1485BC-1431BC) was the Pharaoh that Moses communicated with in approximately 1446 BC. It is believed there were about 2 to 3 million people living around the Nile delta at this time. Many were farmers that were depended on the yearly flooding of the Nile for the land to be fertile for the raising of crops.

SECOND PLAGUE

God directed Moses and Aaron to approach the Pharaoh and again demand that all the Israelites be set free and again Pharaoh refused. God told Moses to request Aaron to stretch out the rod over all the rivers, ponds, streams and cause frogs to come into the homes and cover all the land. This plague caused Pharaoh to take action and requested the presences of Moses and Aaron. He asked that their God would take the frogs away and he would let the Israelites go make sacrifices unto their Lord. Moses spoke to God and asked that the frogs be removed and God responded and removed the frogs. When Pharaoh saw that the frogs were removed he took back his promise (hardened his heart) and refused to let the Israelites go.

THIRD PLAGUE

Exodus 8:16 reads, "And the Lord said unto Moses, Say unto Aaron, Stretch out thy rod, and smite the dust of the land, that it may become lice throughout all the land of Egypt."

The Pharaoh's magicians could not replicate this plague and had to acknowledge that only Moses' God could produce such a miracle.

Exodus: 8:19 reads, "Then the magicians said unto Pharaoh, This is the finger of God: and Pharaoh's heart was hardened, and he hearkened not unto them; as the Lord had said."

Pharaoh still possessed free will and had the resolve to make a decision between good and evil. God hardened the Pharaoh's heart so that his decisions were free of any emotion and not influenced by the plagues. Pharaoh continued to refuse to acknowledge Moses' God and continued to choose evil over good.

Jeremiah 17:9 reads, "The heart is deceitful above all things, and desperately wicked; who can know it?"

God is in effect describing a person's whole being as a heart. It is within this heart that God works within a person to be loving, tender, forgiving, patience, understanding, and sensitive to God's direction. The person can control this heart to be hard, unfeeling, callous, rebellious, bitter, sinful, and reject God's message of love for your neighbor. Pharaoh chose to be evil and reject God's love.

FOURTH PLAGUE

God told Moses once again to rise early and go down to the river and confront Pharaoh.

Exodus 8:20 reads, "And the Lord said unto Moses, rise early in the morning, and stand before Pharaoh: lo, he cometh forth to the water; and say unto him, Thus saith the Lord, Let my people go, that may serve me."

Swarms of flies were sent to Pharaoh's house, his servant's houses, and throughout the country of Egypt except in the land of Goshen where the people of Israel lived. By this time, the county was infested with rotting fish, frogs, and flies that were spreading diseases to both animals and humans. Again, Pharaoh called for Moses and Aaron to discuss a compromise. Again, Pharaoh agreed to let the Israelites go into the desert to make sacrifices to their God. Moses warns Pharaoh not be deceitful. Moses prayed to God for the removal of the flies and God again lifts another plague and removes the flies. Again, Pharaoh did not let the Israelites go due to his willingness to allow evil to control his decision.

FIFTH PLAGUE

This plague was more severe and resulted in the death of all of the Egyptian cattle, horses, camels, sheep, and all other animals. All the animals belonging to the Israelites were not killed. Pharaoh's heart was hardened and refused to let the Israelites go.

SIXTH PLAGUE

Exodus 9:8 reads, "And the Lord said unto Moses and unto Aaron, Take to you handfuls of ashes of the furnace, and let Moses sprinkle it towards the heavens in the sight of Pharaoh."

These ashes were spread by the air throughout all of Egypt and all the Egyptians that breathed the air broke out in boils. Boils covered the Egyptians entire bodies and prevented them from standing.

God continues to prevent Pharaoh from feeling the pressure created by each additional plague. God wants Pharaoh to release his pride to act alone and to knowledge that He is God. God is allowing Pharaohs' decisions to create an example for the entire world and for future worlds how man has free will to choose evil. As we see here, if you choose evil it will lead to complete destruction for you and all those under your direction.

SEVENTH PLAGUE

Once again God speaks to Moses and requests that he approach Pharaoh and say, "Thus saith the Lord God of the Hebrews, Let my people go, that they may serve me".

The plague comes in the form of hail and fire. It destroys all the crops in the field, all the animals in the field, and all the servants in the field. We see at this time there are servants who fear and believe in Moses' God and take shelter for themselves and their cattle. Again, the 600,000 Hebrews in Goshen were protected and did not experience the plague of fire and hail.

At this point we see some change in Pharaoh and his pride. Pharaoh sent for Moses and Aaron and admits he has sinned and that he and servants are wicked.

However, this change in attitude is short lived as he reviews the damage after the fire and hail stops. He cannot control the pride that controls his life and the fear that he may lose control of his kingdom. He has been a god for Egypt and he cannot admit there is a greater God (Yahweh).

EIGHTH PLAGUE

God once again tells Moses to approach Pharaoh and ask him how long he will refuse to humble himself before God.

Exodus 10:3 reads, "And Moses and Aaron came in unto Pharaoh, and said unto him, Thus saith the Lord God of the Hebrews, how long wilt thou refuse to humble thyself before me? Let my people go, that they may serve me."

God tells Moses that he will share this experience with Pharaoh with his children and their children. These signs and plagues will be repeated for generates so that people will understand the importance of recognizing evil (e.g., Pharaoh's pride) and serving and worshiping the Lord God Almighty.

God sends the locust that they may destroy all living plants, trees and fruit. They covered and filled all the houses, destroyed all the plants, trees and all fruits.

Pharaoh's servants begin to complain about the destruction and ask that he let the Hebrews go. Pharaoh again calls for Moses and Aaron and confesses he has sinned against the Lord your God. God removes the locust and the Pharaoh once again refuses to let the Israelites go.

NINTH PLAGUE

The ninth plague came without a warning and the entire country was dark for three days except for the lights in the Israelites homes. The Pharaoh calls for Moses and Aaron and tells them to leave and then changes his mind and refuses to let them go. Pharaoh tells Moses he will die if he sees his face again.

TENTH PLAGUE

God spoke to Moses and told him of the last plague and how to prepare the Israelites for this plague and to be prepared for a fast departure. The tenth plague would bring great pain to the Pharaoh and to all of the Egyptians.

God's instruction to Moses begins by asking him to speak to the Israelites and ask them to get prepared for their departure. Moses' reputation has grown among the Egyptians and many hold him of high esteem. This allows the Israelites to gain favor and borrow provisions from the Egyptians for their journey.

God also provides specific instructions to Moses as to how to be protected from this tenth plague.

Exodus 12:3 reads, "Speak ye unto the congregation of Israel, saying, In the tenth day of this month they shall take to them every man a lamb, according to the house of their fathers, a lamb for a house."

Exodus 12:6–7 reads, "And ye shall keep it up until the fourteenth day of the same month: and the whole assembly of the congregation of Israel shall kill it in the evening. And they shall take of the blood, and strike it on the two side posts and on the upper door post of the houses, wherein they shall eat it."

It should be noted that the calendar used during Moses time was determined by a simple observation of the location of the sun and moon. Today the Jewish calendar is based on mathematical calculations and ritual issues that have added additional time to each year that translates into many days over hundreds of years. The modern calendar we use each day is even further from the astronomical observations used during Moses time. Passover is generally observed in March or April depending on the Jewish calendar. Exodus 12:18 reads, "In the first month, on the fourteenth day of the month at even, ye shall eat unleavened bread, until the one and twentieth day of the month at even."

God provided very specific instruction as to the lamb and unleavened bread.

* The lamb should be shared with your neighbor if there are too few in the house.
* It should be without blemish, a male and less than a year old.
* Each lamb should be separated from all other sheep and goats for 14 days.
* The entire lamb should be consumed by eating or fire.
* Seven days you should eat unleavened bread. This is bread without a raising agent. (Flat Bread).
* No person (stranger) should eat leavened bread during this seven day period.

God's Plan for Moses

This annual Feast of the Passover or the Birth of the nation of Israel should be celebrated by all generations. The message is clear we should be very careful and be aware of the traditions as we remember Passover. God wanted the Israelites to sacrifice their best lamb and to realize the importance of worshiping their God. It was this obedience to God's directions that protected their first born. It was a lesson that was burned into their very souls.

It was the night of the fourteenth day that God smote the first born of all the Egyptians and all the cattle of the Egyptians. Not one Egyptian home was spared from this blanket of death. Pharaoh's first born son was also taken and he responded by calling for Moses and Aaron and demanded that the all the Israelites leave Egypt with all their sheep and cattle.

God was very patient with Pharaoh and requested nine times that the Israelites be released from their bondage. His pride, ego, and refusal to acknowledge the God of the Israelites resulted in the death of all the first born and destroyed Egypt. However, Pharaoh's heart was still hardened and he chased the Israelites to the sea where his army was lost as a wall of water destroyed them all as they tried to cross the sea. After all of these plagues, no man except for Pharaoh could have denied the existence of Moses' God unless they had no feelings or concept of the damage that Egypt endured.

Roman 9:17 reads, "For the scripture saith unto Pharaoh, Even for this same purpose have I raised thee up, that I might show my power in thee, and that my name might be declared throughout all the earth."

Pharaoh was given every opportunity to change his attitude, but refused with his own free will. God used Pharaoh to display his power to all the countries in the region. He is a sovereign God that can show mercy to those he chooses. He raised Pharaoh up for the purpose of showing his power to all the nations for all generations.

Man has always struggled with good and evil. Man has been given free will and has the ability to entertain either good or evil thoughts. He or she's mind (heart) can produce both good and evil thoughts and these thoughts are in many cases diametrically opposed to each other. An evil thought if given consideration may eventually lead to a sinful act. The Holy Spirit provides us with the strength to control our thoughts and to discard evil thoughts. One common method to eliminate evil thoughts is to search God's word for direction and make a determination if an idea or ideas is sin.

Proverbs 4:23 reads, "Keep thy heart with all diligence; for out of it are the issues of life."

Witnesses to a Great Miracle

The Scriptures refers to the heart as the center for all of man's emotions, intellect, and morals. Man has the free will to make decisions that will mold and develop morals, emotions, and intellect. The decisions that one makes will affect them as well as those around them. Pharaoh was an excellent example of a man that allowed sin to control his life and destroy all those around him.

2.

Moses and the Israelites Journey

God continued to speak to Moses as he led the Israelites thought the wilderness for the next forty years. During that 40 years there were many issues and conflicts Moses and Aaron had to resolve. In one situation the Israelites were starving and were making plans to stone Moses and return to Egypt. God intervened and sent food to the Israelites in the form of quails and manna. Again, God was very specific as to how to gather food and when to eat. Again, some people did not follow these laws and commandments and gathered food on the seventh day. God provided manna for the people to eat for the next 40 years.

Leading over 600,000 Israelites for 40 years through the wilderness is a challenge that few men could accomplish. Some estimate the Israelites numbers were close to two million including women, children and others. It was God working through Moses for 40 years that all the Israelites were given food and water and protected from their enemies.

The Amaleks were the first to attack the Israelites as they struggled with the demands of their journey. The Amalek nation had a long history of attacking the weak and those that could not defend themselves. Moses assigned Joshua (Son of Nun from the tribe of Ephraim) to the task of fighting this tribe and destroying their army. Moses with God's staff stood on a nearby mountain to view the battle. Moses held God's staff to the sky for the entire battle with the help of Aaron and Hur. God wanted Joshua and all those involved in battle to realize that it was God who determined who won or lost the battle. We need to be constantly in prayer as we battle the enemy each day. It is those prayers and God's grace that determines if the battle is won or lost. May God have mercy on us if those prayers are not prayed and those hands are not stretched out to heaven.

After the defeat of the Amaleks, the Israelites became increasing dependent on Moses and began to ask him for his blessings and advise for all of their daily activities and problems. When Jethro (Moses father-in-law and priest of Midian) heard of all that was accomplished he rejoiced and provided council to Moses. There were over 600,000 Israelites that were following God's direction through the wilderness and now they all wanted to speak with Moses to learn of God's direction for their individual lives. Jethro recognized the pressure that was being placed on Moses and suggested that Moses choose men that could handle some of the less serious issues. Moses did take Jethro 's advice and formed a judicial court system after the law was given at Mount Sinai. In addition, disputes and grievances were assigned to specific individuals under an organization of men with different levels of responsibilities. However, Moses continued to teach and provide instruction to the Israelites about God's laws and how to live a Godly life. God brought people into Moses life that assisted him carrying out God's purpose and love for the Israelites. We need to be aware that God can bring people into our lives that can assist us in making decisions.

MOUNT SINAI AND A NEW COVENANT

After three months Moses and the Israelites came to Mount Sinai and camped at the foot of the mountain and in the wilderness. God again instructs Moses with the specifics as to how and when to ascend the mountain. God requires Moses to ascend the mount in three days after all the Israelites have washed and have been sanctified.

God loved Moses and the Israelites and wanted them to realize the importance of worshiping Him and loving Him.

Exodus 19:5 reads, "Now therefore, if ye obey my voice indeed, and keep my covenant, then ye shall be a peculiar treasure unto me above all people: for all the earth is mine."

God loves those that obey Him and fear Him. They are God's personal property and they will be protected for all of eternity. God owns the entire world and Israel is God's special treasure.

God then gave to Moses the Ten Commandments that provide them instruction how to live a religious life. Jesus often spoke of the commandments and the importance of obedience.

John 14:23 reads, "Jesus answered and said unto him, If a man love me, he will keep my words: and my Father will love him, and we will come unto him, and make our abode with him"

God's love is dependent on our love for Him and obeying His word.

God chose Moses as the person to receive the Ten Commandments and it was Moses that communicated these commandments to the Hebrew people at the base of Mount Sinai.

Exodus 20:1-17 reads, "And God spake all these words saying. I am the Lord the God, which have brought thee out of the land of Egypt, out of the house of bondage. Thou shalt have no other gods before me. Thou shalt not make unto thee any graven image, or any likeness of any thing that is in heaven above, or that is in the earth beneath, or that is the water under the earth. Thou shalt not bow down thyself to them, nor serve them: for I the Lord the God am a jealous God, visiting the iniquity of the fathers upon the children unto the third and fourth generation of them that hate me.

And showing mercy unto thousands of them that love me, and keep my commandments. Thou shalt not take my name in vain: for the Lord will not hold him guiltless that taketh his name in vain. Remember the Sabbath day, to keep it holy. Six days shalt thou work, and do all thy work. But the seventh day is the Sabbath of the Lord thy God: in it thou shalt not do any work, thou, nor thy son, nor thy daughter, thy manservant, nor thy maidservant, nor thy stranger that is within thy gates. For in six days the Lord made heaven and earth, the sea, and all that in them is, and rested the seventh day: where the Lord blessed the Sabbath day, and hallowed it.

Honor thy father and thy mother: that thy days may be long upon the land which the Lord thy God giveth thee.

Thou shalt not kill.

Thou shalt not commit adultery.

Thou shalt not steal.

Thou shalt not bear false witness against thy neighbor.

Thou shalt not covet thy neighbor's wife, nor his manservant, nor his maidservant, nor his ox, nor his donkey, nor any thing that is thy neighbors."

The Israelites had just escaped from Egypt where they were brutally enslaved for centuries. Exodus 12:41 explains that the Israelites left Egypt after 430 years. They were required to worship all the Egyptian gods and were severely punished if they did not follow all the rituals associated with this worship of Egyptian pagan gods. God heard the Hebrew people cry for release from a bondage that was so severe. The Hebrew people were finally free to follow Moses and worship God, however the worship of idols and gods was a common practice throughout the land for hundreds of years.

The Israelites were weak in their faith in God and quickly returned to the worship of pagan idols when Moses did not return from the Mount Sinai after a few weeks. They molded a calf of gold to worship when they thought Moses was not going to return. They quickly fell back to the state of the natural man and all of natural traits associated with lack of spiritual control. The Ten Commandments provided direction for the Hebrews and how to live a life centered on God's love, mercy, and grace. The Ten Commandments defined sin then and today.

Why did God release the Israelites from their bondage from the Egyptians?

Genesis 12:1–3 reads, "Now the Lord had said unto Abram, Get thee out of thy country, and from thy kindred, and from thy father's house, unto a land that I will show thee: And I will make of thee a great nation, and I will bless thee, and make thy name great: and thou shalt be a blessing: And I will bless them that bless thee, and curse him that curseth thee: and in thee shall all families of the earth be blessed."

God had established a covenant with Abraham and all of his decedents (Israel and its people) with an unconditional promise of a land and blessings. It was Abraham's obedience to God that was the key to unlock blessings for generations. God honored the covenant that He made with Abraham and removed the Israelites from Egypt and guided them through the wilderness.

God also provided an angel that would act as a guide that gave directions to Moses and Aaron.

Exodus 23:20 reads, "Behold, I send an angel before thee, to keep thee in the way, and to bring thee into the place which I have prepared. Beware of him, and obey his voice, provoke him not: for he will not pardon your transgressions: for my name is in him. But if thou shalt indeed obey his voice, and do all that I speak: then I will be an enemy unto thine enemies, and an adversary unto thine adversaries. For mine angel shall go before thee, and bring thee in unto the Amorites, and the Hittites, and the Perizzites, and the Canaanites, and Hivites, and the Jebusites: and I will cut them off."

This angel of the covenant was an angel of great power that could destroy many armies and could bring great fear to anyone that would dare to resist. God tells Moses and Aaron to obey this angel's commands and do not provoke him with any resistance. This angel has God's name within him and represents God's direction.

Jeremiah prophesied (640BC–586BC) that a new covenant would confirm the blessings of the old and the unchangeable laws of God. Under the new covenant God's law would be written on the hearts of man where God's love may be experienced within all man.

Jeremiah 31:31–34 reads, "Behold, the days come, saith the Lord, that I will make a new covenant with the house of Israel, and with the house of Judah. Not according to the covenant that I made with their fathers in the day that I took them by the hand to bring them out of the land of Egypt; which my covenant they brake, although I was a husband unto them, saith the lord: But this shall be the covenant that I will make with the house of Israel; After those days, saith the Lord, I will put my law in their inward parts, and write it in their hearts; and will be their God, and they shall be my people. And they shall teach no more every man his neighbor, and every man his brother, saying, Know the Lord: for they shall all know me, from the least of them unto the greatest of them, saith the Lord: for I will forgive their iniquity, and I will remember their sin no more."

The Israelites had failed during their bondage in Egypt and failed to keep God's law in the wilderness. Christ announced in the upper room that a new covenant would be sealed with His blood on the cross. The new covenant allowed the Holy Spirit to enter into a man's spirit and provide moral direction and a realization of God's mercy and grace. The new covenant was the gift of God's only son Jesus the Savior of all mankind. The forgiveness of all of mans' sin was only possible with the sacrifice of God's greatest gift the death of His only son on the cross.

MOSES' PRAYER FOR THE ISRAELITES

Moses realized that the Israelites were weak in their faith and needed to be continually supported and encouraged. Moses' prayer found in Psalm 90 revealed his depth of insight into mans' natural condition and his many weaknesses.

Moses, in approximately 1440 BC wrote Psalm 90 entitled "From everlasting to everlasting thou art God". Psalm 90:1–6 reads, "Lord, thou hast been our dwelling place in all generations. Before the mountains were brought forth, or ever thou hadst formed the earth and the world, even from everlasting to everlasting, thou art God. Thou turnest man to destruction: and sayest, Return ye children of men. For a thousand years in thy sight are but as yesterday when it is past, and as a watch in the night. Thou carriest them away as with a flood; they are as a sleep: in the morning they are like grass which groweth up. In the morning it flourisheth, and groweth up; in the evening it is cut down, and withereth."

Moses reminds us that God is eternal and that His measure of time is not our understanding of time. We are on this planet for a short period of time and it is important not to waste time on things that are not important.

The Psalm 90:10–12 reads, "The days of our years are threescore years and ten (est. 70 years); and if by reason of strength they be fourscore years (est. 80 years), yet is their strength labor and sorrow; for it is soon cut off and we fly away. Who knoweth the power of thine anger? Even according to thy fear, so is thy wrath. So teach us to number our days, that we may apply our hearts unto wisdom."

We are to be aware of our days and realize that our strength and sorrows are short lived and will pass away. The Israelites struggled for forty years and many did not see the Promised Land, but they remained confident that God was in control and His promises would be fulfilled. We are to be reminded that God's wrath is poured out against sin and that man's natural state is consumed by sin. Man's entire life is under the load of sin and he needs to pray for God's compassion through Jesus Christ our Lord and Savior. We are also on a journey like the Israelites through a wilderness keeping our eyes on the Promised Land that was promised to us by God.

The Psalm 90:15–17 reads, "Make us glad according to the days wherein thou hast afflicted us, and the years wherein we have seen evil. Let thy work appear unto thy servants, and thy glory unto their children. And let the beauty of the Lord our God be upon us: and establish thou the work of our hands upon us: yea, the work of our hands establish thou it."

Moses and the Israelites were in God's plan and were blessed to be part of the journey that was recorded for generations to read and study. God did bring the plagues and the Israelites did see evil, but God's plan did prevail and the Israelites did reach the Promised Land.

Moses as a young man had great love for the Hebrew people, but could not control his violent temperament that resulted in him killing a guard. It wasn't until Moses reached the age of eighty that God began a conversation with Moses that resulted in the release of the Israelites and the journey through the wilderness for the next forty years. God revealed himself through numerous conversations with Moses for forty years between the ages of eighty and one hundred and twenty years. Moses was a man of God that was used by God to unfold His plan for all of mankind.

3.

Moses Experienced God's Wrath

THE ISRAELITES FAILURES WERE great and continued throughout their journey that resulted in the wrath of God. God's wrath is against all sin and will affect all those that are involved in sin. For example, God's wrath was provoked when the Israelites failed to enter into the Promise Land after He had led them out of Egypt and through the wilderness.

Numbers 13:30-32 reads, "And Caleb stilled the people before Moses, and said, Let us go up at once, and possess it; for we are well able to overcome it. But the men that went up with him said, We be not able to go up against the people; for they are stronger than we. And they brought up an evil report of the land which they had searched unto the children of Israel, saying, The land, through which we have gone to search it, is a land that eateth up the inhabitants thereof; and all the people that we saw in it are men of a great stature."

The spies that Moses sent out were afraid of the men they saw in the Promised Land and distorted their report to discourage the Israelites from going forward and obeying God's direction.

The penalty for not obeying God's direction was that Israelites would wander another forty years in the wilderness and that one entire generation would pass away and not see the Promised Land. The consequences of not obeying God's word are severe and needs our full attention. God provides opportunities at specific times and in specific places where we are required to act. God used Caleb to speak the truth and to encourage the people to go forward, but many of the others with Caleb lacked faith. Consequently, evil and fear took control and a report was written that was filled with lies.

Moses was also subject to God's wrath when he struck the rock with his rod in anger. Moses personally struggled controlling his temper his entire life and felt the wrath of God for his actions.

Numbers 20:7–12 reads, "And the Lord spake unto Moses, saying, Take the rod, and gather thou the assembly together, thou and Aaron thy brother, and speak ye unto the rock before their eyes; and it shall give forth his water, and thou shalt bring forth them water out of the rock: so thou shalt give the congregation and their beasts drink. And Moses took the rod from before the Lord, as he commanded him. And Moses and Aaron gather the congregation together before the rock, and he said unto them, Hear now ye rebels; must we fetch you water out of this rock? And Moses lifted up his hand, and with his rod he smote the rock twice: and the water came out abundantly, and the congregation drank, and their beasts also. And the Lord spake unto Moses and Aaron, Because ye believed me not, to sanctify me in the eyes of the children of Israel, therefore ye shall not bring this congregation unto the land which I have given them."

Moses was under a great deal of pressure from the people due to the lack of water and he became impatient and frustrated. God again was specific in his instructions to Moses. He told Moses to hold the rod and to speak to the rock in front of the congregation giving God all the glory. Instead Moses called the Israelites rebels and struck the rock twice with the rod not giving God all the glory. Moses' anger resulted in the disobedience of God's commands and prevented him from entering the Promised Land. Not following God's instructions and not giving God the glory did provoke God's wrath. Moses was a man of God and was able to survive this situation whereas the average man would not.

God is unchanging and never sins. We on the other hand are born of sin and find it difficult not to sin.

ANALYSIS OF MOSES

God loved Moses in spite of his sin and flawed character. His birth and entire life was unique in many ways. It was God's hand that caused Pharaoh's daughter to discover Moses as a baby floating in a basket and then allowing his mother to be his nurse. It was God's hand that caused the Pharaoh's daughter to adopt Moses and raise him in the Pharaoh's palace as a prince. This adoption allowed Moses to receive the best Egypt had to offer (i.e., education, training, food) over a period of 40 years. Living and being part of the Pharaoh's court Moses would have learned many of the skills that were required to lead millions of people. He had firsthand knowledge as to how the Pharaoh and his court operated. God was grooming Moses and developing in him the skills required to be a great leader. As a young man his personality traits were believed to be rough, hot tempered, and a man of action. However, he was also a very passionate man with a strong sense of justice and a love for the Hebrew people.

Hebrews 11:24–26 reads, "By faith Moses, when he was come of years, refused to be called the son of Pharaoh's daughter; Choosing rather to suffer affliction with the people of God, than to enjoy the pleasures of sin for a season; Esteeming the reproach of Christ greater riches than the treasures in Egypt: for he had respect unto the recompense of the reward."

Moses refused to be known as the son of the Pharaoh's daughter and rejected all the power, wealth and prestige associated with being a prince of Egypt. He had a strong character that allowed him to say no to great wealth and say yes to be identified with a group of people that were enslaved. Moses realized that the Pharaoh's power and wealth were only temporary and that he wanted to be part of God's eternal plan and to worship the God of his people the Israelites. At age 40, he witnessed the beating of a Hebrew slave that caused him to lose control and kill the Egyptian guard.

After this incident Moses left Egypt and eventually ended up in Midian a country on the other side of the Sinai Peninsula. It is rationalized that there he married Zipporah a Midianite who was a descendant of Abraham and considered part of the Semitic race. His father-in-law was Jethro a local priest for Midian. Again, we see Moses' sense for justice that causes him to be involved in a dispute over water rights that leads him to Jethro and the marriage to Zipporah. Again, we see how God works with Moses to lead him and prepares him over the next 40 years for the tremendous responsibility of leading an estimated 2 million Israelites out of Egypt. For the next 40 years he learns how to be a husband and a father of two boys and a shepherd of sheep for Jethro. During this time he had to adjust to the idea he was no longer a prince, but a common shepherd dependent on raising sheep as a livelihood. God continues to work with Moses' character as it evolves to include a sense of humility and appreciation for his blessings. It isn't until he reached the age of 80 that God confronts Moses with the task of confronting the Pharaoh and leading the Israelites out of Egypt.

Deuteronomy 34:10 reads, "And there arose not a prophet since in Israel like unto Moses, whom the Lord knew face to face."

Moses knew God; he was the servant of the Lord, and he was filled with the spirit of wisdom. We see how God was working out his plan through Moses as he groomed him, provided him with the skills to lead the Israelites out of Egypt, and to deliver the Ten Commandments as a New Covenant.

It was Joshua that finally led the Israelites into the Promised Land after the death of Moses and Aaron in about 1450 BC. In the next seven years was a complex process that involved a number of conflicts with the Canaanites over land as Joshua made the determinations as which tribe would receive which parcel of land. In some cases, the Jordan River acted as a dividing border for many of the 12 tribes. The land parcels for the tribe of Asher and Naphtali were the northern part of Israel from the Mediterranean Sea to the Jordan River. The southern portions of land were occupied by the tribes of Judah and Simeon bordered by the Dead Sea with the Philistines to the west. The land between these portions were occupied by the tribes of Zebulon, Isaacher, Manasseh, Dan, Ephraim, Gad, Benjamin, and Reuben.

At a much later date the conquering Romans renamed the Land of Israel as Palestine in an attempt to discredit the Jews and not recognize their claim to the Promised Land of Israel. The immigration of Arab people to the area occurred at a much later date.

4.

Elijah

THE NAME ELIJAH MEANS "My God is Yahweh." It is estimated he was born in 900 BC at Tishba in the Gilead region (located in the northern kingdom of Israel) during the time of King Ahab and King Ahaziah. It was said, he was born with an angel at his side that provided a fabric of fire that surrounded him. We are told his appearance was rough due to the fact he lived off the land and would rest in caves. However, he had a relationship with God that few men have ever experienced. As a Jewish priest, Elijah lived a life in complete obedience to God's will that resulted in him seeing and prophesying events that were impossible to be foreseen by any other human being. He grew to be one of the most important prophets in the world and experienced first-hand blessing directly from God.

God used Elijah as a prophet to reveal and communicate His purpose in reflecting His divine glory.

Deuteronomy 18:18–19 reads, "I will raise them up a Prophet from among their brethren, like unto thee, and will put my words in his mouth; and he shall speak unto them all that I shall command him. And it shall come to pass, that whosoever will not hearken unto my words which he shall speak in my name, I will require it of him."

God raised up many prophets among the people for the purpose of providing an intercessor between God and man. Like Moses, God spoke directly to Elijah and directed him as to what to say to King Ahab.

The prophets are classified by the length and scope of the book. The Major Prophets were Isaiah, Jeremiah, and Ezekiel. The twelve Minor Prophets are Hosea, Joel, Amos, Obadiah, Jonah, Micah, Nahum, Habakkuk, Zephaniah, Haggai, Zechariah, and Malachi. Elijah was neither a major nor minor prophet due to the lack of written records. However, Elijah held a prominent position as a prophet due to his unparalleled relationship with God and His divine plan for mankind.

ELIJAH'S PROPHECY

Elijah's first recorded prophecy is found in 1 Kings 17:1, which reads, "And Elijah the Tishbite, who was the inhabitants of Gilead, said unto Ahab, As the Lord God of Israel liveth, before whom I stand , there shall not be dew nor rain these years , but according to my word."

Ahab the king and his wife Jezebel wanted to replace the worship of God (Yahweh) with the worship of Baal, the pagan god of rain, fertility, and the provider of children, and crops. There were also many other gods that were worshiped during this time for numerous reasons. Elijah heard of the King's intensions to force the people to worship pagan gods and became enraged that such a disgraceful act would be intentioned.

Elijah traveled to Samaria and delivered the ultimatum to Ahab that a drought would be realized due their decision to worship Baal rather than God. It is believed that Ahab mocked Elijah and said he paid homage to all of the gods and enjoyed all the good things of this earth. The drought began as Elijah had prophesied and King Ahab became enraged and began seeking out Elijah to kill him. Elijah literality fled for his life and lived off the land, and was protected by God.

1 Kings 17:2–4 reads, "And the word of the Lord came unto him, saying, Get thee hence, and turn thee eastward, and hide thyself by the brook Cherith, that is before Jordan. And it shall be, that thou shalt drink of the brook; and I have commanded the ravens to feed thee there."

God used ravens to feed Elijah both in the morning and evening as he hid in a ravine east of the Jordan River near the brook Cherith. He was there for some time until the brook began to dry up due to the drought and God told him to travel to the city of Zaraphath on the Mediterranean coast at a distance of more than 70 miles. There he met a poor widow that recognized him as an Israelite and provided food to Elijah.

1 Kings 17:12–15 reads, "And she said, As the Lord thy God liveth, I have not a cake, but a handful of meal in a barrel, and a little oil in a cruse: and, behold, I am gathering two sticks, that I may go in and dress it for me and my son, that we may eat it, and die. And Elijah said unto her, fear not; go and do as thou hast said; but make me thereof a little cake first, and bring

it unto me, and after make for thee and for thy son. For thus saith the Lord God of Israel, The barrel of meal shall not waste, neither shall the cruse of oil fail, until the day that the Lord sendeth rain upon the earth. And she went and did according to the saying of Elijah: and she, and he, and her house, did eat many days."

God used a poor Gentile woman to reveal His divine love and grace. This woman was willing to give all her food that would have resulted in the starvation for herself and her son. God blessed this gift and multiplied it to provide enough food for Elijah, the woman and her son, for the remainder of the drought. This Gentile woman's faith and obedience was blessed and honored by God.

God spoke to Elijah again after the three years of famine and told him to show himself to Ahab the seventh king of Israel (873BC to 853BC). Jezebel the queen and wife of Ahab convinced Ahab to build a temple to Baal and oppose the worship of the God of the Hebrew people. She wanted all the prophets of the Hebrew God to be killed.

Jezebel was a Phoenician, a sea fairing people that occupied the city of Tyre and Sidon located on the Mediterranean Sea north of Israel. She was deeply involved in the worship of Baal with 450 priests and Ashtoreth with 400 priests. She was also fanatical in spending a great deal of time and money in building temples for these pagan gods. Her father was a king and also a high priest for these gods.

Jeremiah19:5 reads, "They have built also the high place of Baal, to burn their sons with fire for burnt offerings unto Baal, which I commanded not, nor spake it, neither came it into my mind."

The worshipers of Baal had reached new depths of immorality as they scarified their own children to gain favor with the gods. It was a common belief that one's success or failure in life was dependent on the gods and how they accepted or rejected their sacrifices.

At this point God tells Elijah to gather all the people on Mount Carmel for a test of the pagan gods.

1Kings 18:18–19 reads, "And he answered, I have not troubled Israel; but thou, and thy father's house, in that ye have forsaken the commandments of the Lord, and thou hast followed Baalim. Now therefore send, and gather to me all Israel unto Mount Carmel, and the prophets of Baal four hundred and fifty, and the prophets of the groves four hundred, which eat at Jezebel's table."

God blessed Elijah with great courage as he stood alone on Mount Carmel against hundreds that would love to discredit him and kill him. Elijah stood before them all and challenged them all not to worship two gods, but to make a decision which god was the false god. They needed to make a decision between worshiping Baal and worshiping the true God of the Hebrews.

I King 18:24 reads, "And call ye on the name of your gods, and I will call on the name of the Lord: and the God that answereth by fire, let him be God. And all the people answered and said, It is well Spoken."

The 450 prophets of Baal and others called upon Baal from morning till noon and no voice was heard and no fire was seen. Elijah began to mock them and said they need to cry loader because Baal must be busy or sleeping. Elijah asked them to come closer to see as he repaired the altar of the Lord that was broken down. Elijah took twelve stones that would represent the twelve tribes and covenant the Lord made with the Hebrew people and dug a trench around the altar. He then pilled wood and placed the sacrifice on top. After, he poured four barrels of water on the wood and then repeated the pouring of water until the drench around the altar was filled.

I Kings 18:36–39 reads, "And it came to pass at the time of the offering of the evening sacrifice, that Elijah the prophet came near, and said, Lord God of Abraham, Isaac, and of Israel, let it be known this day that thou art God in Israel, and that I am thy servant, and that I have done all these things at thy word. Hear me, O Lord, hear me, that this people may know that thou art the Lord God, and that thou hast turned their hearts back again. Then the fire of the Lord fell, and consumed the burnt sacrifice, and the wood, and the stones, and the dust, and licked up the water that was in the trench. And when all the people saw it, they fell on their faces: and they said, The Lord, he is the God; the Lord, he is the God."

There are a number of similarities between Moses and Elijah. God himself spoke through both Moses and Elijah. God blessed both men with the courage and confidence to challenge rulers that could have taken their lives for any reason. They were both highly sensitive and obedient to God's word. They both lived their lives completely depend on God for direction. God worked miracles through these men to communicate His message and further His kingdom.

God not only sent fires to consume the complete altar of the Lord on Mount Carmel, but He also delivered a death sentence to the prophets of Baal. The lives of the prophets of Baal were all destroyed. The sentence for worshiping false gods was death. Today we see many that worship many false gods. Their first priority is not to worship our God and Savior, but to accumulate wealth or things, gain recognition or status, consume food, drink, or drugs. These are Satan's priorities that lead to greed, jealousy, killing, hatred for one another, and a complete breakdown of society.

Elijah was under God protection, but at times had to run with God's direction for his life as those such as Jezebel sought to kill him. As Elijah, Christians need not to walk from evil, but to run from evil. There are many Jezebels that are still eager to destroy Christian lives, their values, and their families. We see Jezebels today as they try to convince our children to buy into their pagan life style of sexual perversion and love of self. Living a moral, ethical life requires one to recognize that God is our creator and that He requires us to worship Him and to live a life that is obedient to His laws. God sent His only Son who paid the price for all our sins, if we accept Him and believe in Him.

When Jezebel heard of the death of her 450 prophets of Baal she became enraged and sent a message to Elijah telling him of her intension to end his life. Elijah left the area and traveled to Beer-sheba within Judah where he left his servants. He then continued his journey into the wilderness where he found rest under a juniper tree.

1 Kings 19:5–7 reads, "And as he lay and slept under a juniper tree, behold then an angel touched him, and said unto him, Arise and eat. And he looked, and behold, there was a cake baked on the coals, and a cruse of water at his head. And he did eat and drink, and laid him down again. And the angel of the Lord came gain the second time, and touched him, and said, Arise and eat; because the journey is too great for thee."

In the last few days Elijah had experienced God's great power in the consuming by fire of the altar that he had built for God and the killing all of the 450 false prophets of Baal. However, fear took control of Elijah after getting the message from Jezebel and the threat to take his life. Elijah had experienced the emotional high of God's great power firsthand with the pouring of fire from the heavens, the answer to his prayers for rain, and the elimination of 450 false prophets. Just after all these great things have been accomplished Elijah gets a death notice from Jezebel (Satan incarnate). After all that had transpired, he does not understand why he is still in a battle with Satan and the people are still consumed with idol worship. Elijah was exhausted and discouraged and asked God to take his life. Again, God was faithful and sent angels to minister to Elijah and prepare him for another journey.

Elijah's experience with great success and then with failure is common today as people are swept away at times from great joy only to fall later to great depression. We see great successes as churches grow with great faith and then falter as something else grabs their attention. The struggle between good and evil is a daily struggle that requires constant prayer and thanksgiving.

As Moses, Elijah travels through the wilderness with God's direction and His angels. For 40 days and 40 nights he traveled to Mount Horeb in the Sinai. It is believed this is the same place where God made his covenant with Israel and gave Moses the 10 commandments.

1 Kings 19:9–11 reads, "And he came thither unto a cave, and lodged there; behold, the word of the Lord came to him, and he said unto him, What doest thou here, Elijah? And he said, I have been very jealous for the Lord God of hosts: for the children of Israel have forsaken thy covenant, thrown down thine altars, and slain thy prophets with the sword; and I, even I only, am left; and they seek my life, to take it away."

God asked Elijah what he was doing in this cave as if to say there is much to be done and this was not the way to get His work accomplished. God was very patient and loving with His servant and knew what he had experienced. The Lord is merciful, gracious, longsuffering, and is full of goodness and truth.

1Kings 19:15–16 reads, "And the Lord said unto him, Go, return on thy way to the wilderness of Damascus: and when thou comest, anoint Hazael to be King over Syria. And Jehu the son of Nimshi shalt thou anoint to be king over Israel: and Elisha the son of Shaphat of Abel-meholah shalt thou anoint to be prophet in thy room."

God explained to Elijah he had a great deal of traveling and work to complete. He had to return back to the wilderness and travel hundreds of miles to Damascus to anoint a new King over Syria and to anoint a new King over Israel. On his travels he would also meet Elisha who would eventually replace Elijah as the new prophet to Israel.

At this point, Israel and the Jewish people had a number of enemies in the area that would like to invade Israel and steal her treasures and land. Benhadad the king of Syria (885BC-860BC) had a great army and the support of 32 other kings in the area. King Benhadad was jealous of Israel's riches and wanted Samaria and its rich land and sent a messenger to King

Ahab demanding that King Ahad turn over all his gold and property. King Benhadad and the people of Syria worshiped a number of pagan gods and were greatly dependent on hundreds of false prophets for direction in many areas of their lives. However, God sends an unnamed prophet of God to King Ahab of Israel to explain that God would not allow his army to be defeated by the Syrians. The fact that this prophet told Ahad what was going to happen, makes it impossible for Ahab not to acknowledge it was God who was in control of the outcome of this war. God saved King Ahad from a certain defeat and death. God wanted Ahab and all men to acknowledge that God was control and to place their trust in Him and not on themselves.

Ahab is also involved in a conflict over a vineyard owned by Naboth. The vineyard was located in Jezreel next to Ahab's palace in Samaria. Ahad wanted to purchase the vineyard, but Naboth refused because it was promised as part of a family inheritance. Ahad was displeased and complained to Jezebel. Jezebel (Satan incarnate) developed a scheme that would place Naboth in a very difficult position. Jezebel paid for witnesses that claimed that Naboth had blasphemed God and the king. The people when they heard of this blasphemy claim took Naboth out of the city and stoned him to death. Due to custom Naboth sons were also killed thereby allowing the King to lay claim to the vineyard.

As with Moses, God required Elijah to confront the ruler of the land, in this case Ahad King of Israel. Elijah found Ahad in the vineyard of Naboth whom he killed with Jezebel's scheme.

1 Kings 21:17-20 reads, "And the word of the Lord came to Elijah the Tishbite, saying, Arise, go down to meet Ahad king of Israel, which is in Samaria: behold, he is in the vineyard of Naboth, whither he is gone down to possess it. And thou shalt speak unto him, saying, Thus saith the Lord, Hast thou killed, and also taken possession? And thou shalt speak unto him, saying, "Thus saith the Lord, In the place where dogs licked the blood of Naboth shall dogs lick thy blood, even thine. And Ahab said to Elijah, Hast thou found me, O mine enemy? And he answered, I have found thee: because thou hast sold thyself to work evil in the sight of the Lord."

1 Kings 21:28–29 reads, "And the word of the Lord came to Elijah the Tishbite, saying. Seest thou how Ahab humbleth himself before me? because he humbleth himself before me, I will not bring the evil in his days: but in his son's days will I bring the evil upon his house."

God was instructing Elijah by saying He will determine how, when, and where Ahab will be confronted by his sins. God is in control and he will determine when evil is released and the penalty for sin is paid. In this case, because Ahab had repented and publically displayed his remorse God did provide a temporary stay. However, Ahab was later killed and his sins were transferred to his sons who were also killed. Confession of our sins and praying for our forgiveness is important aspect of being a Christian.

Christians today are under God's grace due to His overwhelming love, love we are not worthy of, and a love we cannot comprehend. God allowed His only Son to die on a cross to give all of mankind the opportunity to spend eternity with Him in heaven. Today we are dependent on the Holy Spirit to help us to recognize our sins and make changes that will place us in communion with our Creator.

After the death of King Ahab, Ahaziah his son assumed control of northern Israel and Jehoshaphat maintains control over Judah. The death of a King would normally leave some vacuum in control and rebellion would normally break out. Mesha king of Moab (area east of the Dead Sea and now western Jordan) was successful in a rebellion over high taxes. Ahaziah became sick and requested an oracle of Baal that was a rebellion to the worship of the God of Israel. It was this rebellion by King Ahaziah and the following of his mother (Jezebel) in the worship of Baal that provoked the anger of the Lord God of Israel.

2 Kings 1:3–4 reads, "But the angel of the Lord said to Elijah the Tishbite, Arise, go up to meet the messengers of the King of Samaria, and say unto them, Is it not because there is not a God in Israel, that ye go to inquire of Baal-zebub the god of Ekron? Now therefore thus saith the Lord, Thou shalt not come down from that bed on which thou art gone up, but shalt surely die. And Elijah departed."

The angel of the Lord speaks directly to Elijah as he did with Moses and commands him to confront King Ahaziah. The angel of the Lord speaks as God, executes the power of God, and identifies himself as God. Those that see him fear for their lives because they recognize the power and presences of God himself. King Ahaziah had deliberately turned from the Lord God of Israel and worshiped Baal for the healing of his aliment. His worship of Baal was responsible for hardening the hearts of the people against the God of Israel.

King Ahaziah sends 50 soldiers after Elijah to punish him for confronting the King of Israel about his idol worship and demand that he repent as did his father Ahab.

2 Kings 1:12 reads, "And Elijah answered and said unto them, If I be man of God, let fire come down from heaven, and consume thee and thy fifty. And the fire of God came down from heaven, and consumed him and his fifty."

God did work directly through Elijah to deliver His words and response to King Ahaziah's decision to worship pagan idols. God's message was clear when fire poured down to destroy two units of 50 soldiers and His decision to let King Ahaziah die in his bed from his own aliments.

The death of King Ahaziah resulted in Jehoram becoming King of Israel. It is believed that King Jehoram (852BC to 841BC) was the brother of Ahab and was King of the northern kingdom after the death of King Ahaziah.

God at this time reveals to Elijah that he will soon depart from this earth and needs to prepare Elisha to take his place. Elisha's main task would be to carry on Elijah's mission to stop the worship of idols. Elisha then asked Elijah to provide him with a double portion of his spiritual power and understanding. Obviously, this is only possible through God's will.

Elijah's reputation was great among the prophets and he shared his vision with the guild of prophets and priests of Israel. This guild of 50 prophets began to follow Elijah at a distance to both provide protection and to bear witness to the prophecy of his departure.

We are limited in our ability to understand all of God's plans and actions that take place within a man's life here on earth and in heaven. This was especially true of Elijah who like Moses spoke directly with God. Elijah was an extraordinary man that had an extraordinary relationship with God Almighty. He was chosen of God to be His representative and experienced God's protection and care.

2 Kings 2:11 reads, "And it came to pass, as they still went on, and talked, that, behold, there appeared a chariot of fire, and horses of fire, and parted them both asunder; and Elijah went up by a whirlwind into heaven."

God is in control and He will decide what will transpire on earth and within each man's life. In this case, God decided that it was time for Elijah to depart this earth and go to heaven, so He took him. At this time, God determined the mission of confronting the pagan idol worshipers would be passed on to Elisha. So the mission and the mantle were then passed on to Elisha.

Elijah was a man with many human frailties, but his heart and soul was devoted completely to the worship and praise of the Lord God Almighty of Israel. The governments, its rules, were all corrupt and wanted to continue to enslave it's people to worship Baal and other idols for the purpose of extorting money and other valuables for the promise of good fortune. God knew the heart of Elijah and accepted him as His messenger to deliver God's voice to a people that were lost in the worship of pagan idols.

ANALYSIS OF ELIJAH

God loved Elijah regardless of his many human frailties. His life was at times completely dependent of God for food, shelter, and protection. His single purpose in life was to please God with His prophecies. He was God's messenger and His humble obedient servant. He was truly a unique individual that lived off the land and took shelter wherever God provided it.

Society and the culture of that day had fallen to great depths. It was common for people to worship idols in the hope of receiving a good crop and healthy animals. Their superstitions made them easy prey for corrupt rulers like King Ahab and Jezebel who promoted this worship of pagan gods by building monuments and temples for Baal and others. In addition, hundreds of priests and oracles were employed to convince people to sacrifice animals, money, and children to these false gods for rain, sun, and prosperity.

5.

Peter the Apostle

PETER (SIMON) THE APOSTLE (1 BC to 64 AD) had one brother Andrew who also became an Apostle and a follower of Jesus the Christ. It is believed Peter wrote the Gospel of Mark with the assistance of John Mark. It is also generally believed he wrote the First and Second Epistle of Peter. He was a fisherman with little formal education, lived in the village of Bethsaida, and worked in Capernaum with fishing nets on the Sea of Galilee. He was married, worked with his father (Jona) and brother, Andrew in a physically demanding job with long hours. Generally, Simon was considered to be an outspoken man that felt free to share his opinions and at times a little rough around the edges. The area was considered to be in extreme poverty with a strong sense of independence from Jerusalem.

The first mention of Simon (Peter) is after Jesus is baptized on the Jordan River south of the Sea of Galilee. It appears both Peter and Andrew were both associated with John the Baptist and his ministry. When John the Baptist met Jesus he knew who Jesus was and immediately called Him the Lamb of God. It is also possible that John the Baptist may have been aware of Jesus of Nazareth from relatives and other acquaintances. It should be noted Peter, Andrew and Jesus were about around 30 years of age with Andrew being the youngest.

John 1:35-42 reads, "Again the next day after John stood, and two of his disciples; And looking upon Jesus as he walked, he saith, Behold the Lamb of God! And two disciples heard him speak, and they followed Jesus. And Jesus turned, and saw them following, and saith unto them, What seek ye? They said unto him, Rabbi, (which is to say, being interpreted, Master,) where dwellest thou? He saith unto them, Come and see. They came and

Witnesses to a Great Miracle

saw where he dwelt, and abode with him that day: for it was about the tenth hour. One of the two which heard John speak, and followed him, was Andrew, Simon Peter's brother. He first findeth his own brother Simon, and saith unto him, We have found the Messiah, which is, being interpreted, the Christ. And he brought him to Jesus. And when Jesus beheld him, he said, Thou art Simon the son of Jona, thou shalt be called Cephas, which is by interpretation Peter or rock."

This first meeting between Peter, Andrew and Jesus resulted in Andrew and Peter deciding to become more involved with the ministry of Jesus of Nazareth. Jesus knows Simon (Peter) and knows Peter will be a leader for the Apostle and the foundation of Christ's church.

The next time we learn of Simon (Peter) he is in Capernaum or Bethsaida fishing with his partners the sons of Zebedee, John and James.

Luke 5:1–10 reads, "And it came to pass, that, as the people pressed upon him to hear the word of God, he stood by the lake of Gennesaret. And saw two ships standing by the lake: but the fishermen were gone out of them, and were washing their nets. And he entered into one of the ships, which were Simon's, and prayed him that he would thrust out a little from the land. And he sat down, and taught the people out of the ship. Now when he had left speaking, he said unto Simon, Launch out into the deep, and let down your nets for a draught. And Simon answering said unto him, Master, we have toiled all night, and have taken nothing: nevertheless at thy word I will let down the net. And when they had this done, they enclosed a great multitude of fishes: and their net brake. And they beckoned unto their partners, which were in the other ship, that they should come and help them. And they came, and filled both ships, so that they began to sink. When Simon Peter saw it he fell down at Jesus' knees, saying, Depart from me; for I am a sinful man, O Lord. For he was astonished, and all that were with him, at the draught of the fishes which they had taken: And so was also James, and John, the sons of Zebedee, which were partners with Simon. And Jesus said unto Simon, Fear not; from henceforth thou shalt catch men."

At this time Jesus steps into Peter's boat due to the crowds of people and asks Peter to take them out a few feet so that He may continue to preach to the people on the shore. Jesus continues His preaching of the gospel as Simon Peter listens. After which, Jesus tells Peter to move his boat out to deeper water and cast his nets. Peter explains he had fished all night and there were no fish to be caught. However, Peter obeys Jesus' wishes and goes out to deeper water and lets down his nets. And, to his surprise he nets so many fish that he asks John and James to bring out their boat to help pull in all the fish. Both boats worked together landing the fish to the point to where both boats began to sink. The reality of the situation hits Peter hard to the point to where he realizes he is in presence of a miracle and God's messenger. Peter falls at the feet of Jesus and asks that Jesus leave him due to the sin in his life. He feels he is not worthy to be in the presence of Jesus and asks that Jesus depart from him. Satan (fallen man, natural man) is at work with Peter trying to convince him not to follow Jesus because of his sin. Peter physically was a strong man capable of pulling in large heavy nets filled with fish, but spiritually he was weak and was overcome by fear of failure. Jesus knew that Peter would grow to be a great disciple and continued to love him and work with him regardless of his human frailties. God shows that same love and patience today as we wrestle with fear and strive to grow in faith.

Next we find Jesus at Peter's mother-in-law's house. She is sick and needs immediate attention.

Luke 4:38–39 reads, "And he arose out of the synagogue, and entered into Simon's house. And, Simon's wife's mother was taken with a great fever; and they besought him for her. And he stood over her, and rebuked the fever; and it left her: and immediately she arose and ministered unto them."

Peter is present with Jesus as He rebukes the fever and allows Peter's wife's mother to continue with her life. As they continue their travels Peter's knowledge and understanding of Jesus' ministry grows stronger to the point Peter becomes the lead apostle.

Mark 3:13–19 reads, "And he goeth up into a mountain, and calleth unto him whom he would and they came unto him. And he ordained twelve, that they should be with him, and that he might send them forth to preach. And to have power to heal sicknesses, and to cast out devils; And Simon the surnamed Peter; And James the son of Zebedee, and John the brother of James; and he surnamed them Boanerges, which is, the sons of thunder. And Andrew, and Philip, and Bartholomew, and Matthew, and Thomas, and James the son of Alphaeus, and Thaddeus, and Simon the Canaanite, And Judas Iscariot, which also betrayed him: and they went into a house."

Jesus goes to the mountain to pray and make the decision as to who would be ordained to be His disciples. Simon Peter is the first to be considered and the first to be ordained to be one of Jesus' disciples. Obviously, Peter is held in high regard as a leader and that Jesus would delegate great responsibility and power to heal the sick and cast out demons. Peter was a follower who was eager to learn and who was quick to assume more responsibility over the next two years.

God had a covenant with the Jewish people and wanted to ensure that they were the first to hear the good news that Jesus was the Messiah. Peter and the disciples first mission was to go out into the Jewish community by twos to preach that Jesus was the Messiah, heal the sick, and cast out demons. Peter leads the disciples as they travel from village to village preaching that Jesus is the Messiah.

Mark 5:37–43 reads, "And he suffered no man to follow him, save Peter, and James, and John the brother of James. And he cometh to the house of the ruler of the synagogue, and seeth the tumult, and them that wept and wailed greatly. And when he was come in, he said unto them, Why make ye this ado, and weep? The damsel is not dead, but sleepeth." And they laughed him to scron. But when he had put them all out, he taketh the father and the mother of the damsel, and them that were with him, and entereth in where the damsel was lying. And he took the damsel by the hand, and said unto her, "Talitha cumi"; which is, being interpreted, "Damsel", (I say unto thee,) "arise". And straightway the damsel arose, and walked, for she was of the age of twelve years. And they were astonished with a great astonishment. And he charged them straitly that no man should know it; and commanded that something should be given her to eat."

Jesus required that Peter, James, and John be present at this miracle for their own enrichment and for a number of other reasons. These Apostles had to experience and realize the full impact that Jesus was God and that God has power over sin, disease, death, and Satan. They were to act as witnesses to Jesus' Transfiguration and later to Jesus' Ascension. There is no limitation to God's power and the disciples needed to realize that this power was available through faith. The miracles that Jesus completed were in the presence of faith, for building faith, and for proclaiming that Jesus was the Messiah.

A transformation took place within Peter that changed him from an outspoken rough man of thunder, to a humble obedient servant of the Lord God Almighty even to death. He rejoiced the day of his death that he would now be reunited with his Savior that had been crucified over 30 years prior.

Matthew 16:13–16 reads, "When Jesus came into the coasts of Caesarea Philippi, he asked his disciples, saying, Whom do men say that I the Son of man am? And they said, Some say that thou art John the Baptist: some, Elijah; and others, Jeremiah, or one of the prophets. He saith unto them, But whom say ye that I am? And Simon Peter answered and said, Thou art the Christ, the Son of the living God. And Jesus answered and said unto him, Blessed art thou, Simon Bar-jona: for flesh and blood hath not revealed it unto thee, but my Father which is in heaven. And I say also unto thee, That thou art Peter, and upon this rock I will build my church; and the gates of hell shall not prevail against it. And I will give unto thee the keys of the kingdom of heaven: and whatsoever thou shalt bind on earth shall be bond in heaven: and whatsoever thou shalt loose on earth shall be loosed in heaven."

Caesarea Philippi is a city located about 120 miles northeast of Jerusalem at the foot of Mount Hermon. The location provides a contrast between Jesus the Messiah and the local culture that is buried in the superstition and acts of pure evil related to the worship of many gods. Herod the Great built a temple near the Mount to celebrate Caesar Augustus, hence the name Caesarea Philippi. Jesus takes the disciples on the 25 mile journey from Galilee to Caesarea Philippi for the purpose allowing them to be free of the daily distractions and to concentrate on their mission with Jesus. When Jesus asked the question, "But whom say ye that I am?" It is only Peter that responses without hesitation and said, "Thou art the Christ, the Son of the living God." It was Peter that reached that level of spiritual discernment and allowed him to freely identify Jesus' deity as being God's Son.

God blessed Peter throughout his life for his faith, for his discernment, and for his unwavering faithfulness. It was Peter and his testimony that God used as the rock that lead the disciples and provided a foundation for the church. Jesus is the Messiah and through Him God is keeping His promise to provide a Savior for all of mankind as was prophesied. God at this point is giving Peter more responsibility and authority for building the church.

God promised to give Peter the keys to heaven that will allow him to enter heaven. This was only possible because of his confession of faith and the confession of faith by all the Apostles. The confession of faith also resulted in God also giving Peter and the Apostles the authority to bind and loose the church with respect to daily issues that needed to be addressed. Jesus left Peter and the Apostles on earth with God's authority to continue to build the church and to preach that God gave the ultimate sacrifice for our sins and that was the life of His only Son, Jesus. Confession of faith by man is the only possible way to spend eternity with your Creator.

Roman rule over Israel was severe and the penalty for a convicted criminal was death on a cross. The convicted criminal was required to carry their cross to the place of crucifixion. This was a long and painful death that may last three or four days. To the common man at that time the cross meant only one thing, a long and painful death. Peter may have thought Jesus was there to rescue them from this oppressive Roman rule and become king of Israel.

Consequently, when Peter heard Jesus explain he was going to die and rise on the third day he was bewildered. Peter was a bold and impetuous Apostle who did not hesitate to challenge Jesus when he spoke of His own death.

Matthew 16:22-23 reads, "Then Peter took Him, and began to rebuke him, saying, Be it far from thee, Lord: this shall and be unto thee. But he turned, and said unto Peter, Get thee behind me, Satan: for thou savorest not the things that be of God, thou those that be of men."

Peter's reaction reveals that he did not fully understand the purpose for Jesus' death and resurrection. Peter is going through a transformation from a natural man with many frailties to a spiritual man. Jesus sees that Satan is once again trying to tempt Him from carrying out God's promise to provide salvation for all of mankind. Jesus was also teaching that there is a cost related to discipleship and that cost may involve losing your life.

Matthew 16:24 reads, "Then said Jesus unto his disciples, If any man will come after me, let him deny himself, and take up his cross, and follow me."

Jesus was telling his disciples that they need to realize that there is a cost related to following Him. Peter and the Apostles were learning that following Jesus would involve a cost and part of that cost would be to deny self.

Jesus, Peter, and the disciples travel to Jerusalem where the final days unfold of Jesus' life.

Matthew 26:40 reads, "And he cometh unto the disciples, and findeth them asleep, and saith unto Peter, What, could ye not watch with me one hour?"

Gethsemane was a beautiful garden on the slopes of the Mount of Olives that was used as a place for rest and reflection. It was a perfect place for Jesus, Peter, and the disciples to pray. Peter and the disciples again showed their human weakness when Jesus finds them sleeping rather than praying.

Even during this final hour of greatest need, Peter fails to keep watch and pray.

During this late hour of darkness Judas, Malchus (servant of the high priest), and a number of the soldiers slithered into the gardens to betray and arrest Jesus.

John 18:10 reads, "Then Simon Peter having a sword drew it, and smote the high priest's servant, and cut off his right ear. The servant's name was Malchus."

Peter again was quick to react and was willing to defend Jesus with his sword. He was highly capable physically and knows how to defend himself and Jesus with a sword. Peter was capable of being very loyal to Jesus, but at times rash and hasty. It seems his formal training was limited and he made mistakes at times, but he assumes great responsibility readily and has natural leadership skills.

One of Peter's greatest failures is when he denies Jesus three times.

Mark 14:66–72 reads, "And as Peter was beneath in the place, there cometh one of the maids of the high priest. And when she saw Peter warming himself, she looked upon him, and said, And thou also was with Jesus of Nazareth. But he denied, saying, I know not, neither understand I what thou sayest. And he went out into the porch; and the cock crew. And a maid saw him again, and began to say to them that stood by, This is one of them. And he denied it again, And a little after, they that stood by said again to Peter, Surely thou art one of them: for thou art a Galilean, and thy speech thereto. But he began to curse and to swear, saying, I know not this man of whom ye speak. And the second time the cock crew. And Peter called to mind the word that Jesus said unto him, Before the cock crew twice, thou shalt deny me thrice. And when he thought thereon, he wept."

Peter was present as the high priest began to question Jesus at the place. Peter sat with the servants so as not to be detected and to listen and watch the hearing conducted by the Sanhedrin. The witnesses against Jesus were for the most part conflicting and not enough to convict Jesus of any crime. However, the high priest began to ask Jesus if he was the Christ the Son of the Blessed. Until this point Jesus had said nothing.

Mark 14:62 reads, "And Jesus said, I am: and ye shall see the Son of man sitting on the right hand of power, and coming in the clouds of heaven."

Jesus in this statement provides the information that is needed to convict him of blasphemy and the death penalty. Peter was listening intently and must have been completely demoralized when he heard Jesus speak and the sentence of death that was issued. Peter could no longer protect his Savior with his might and sword. Fear (Satan) took hold and Peter tried to hide in the crowds, however, he was spotted and questioned a few times if he was a follower of Jesus. His desire to survive overtook him and he lied that he did not know Jesus three times before the cock crow twice. At that moment in time Peter recalled what Jesus had said and he left and wept bitterly.

After the crucifixion, Peter and the other disciples were in great distress and in hiding not sure if they would be next. Mary of Magdala was the first at the grave site in the early morning hours.

John 20:1–7 reads, "The first day of the week cometh Mary Magdalene early, when it was yet dark, unto the sepulcher, and seeth the stone taken away from the sepulcher. Then she runneth, and cometh to Simon Peter, and to the other disciple, whom Jesus loved, and said unto them, They have taken away the Lord out of the sepulcher, and we know not where they have laid him. Peter therefore went forth, and that other disciple, and came to the sepulcher. So they ran both together: and the other disciples did outrun Peter, and came first to the sepulcher. And he stooping down, and looking in, saw the linen clothes lying; yet went he not in. Then cometh Simon Peter following him, and went into the sepulcher, and seeth the linen clothes lie. And the napkin, that was about his head, not lying with the linen clothes, but wrapped together in a place by itself."

After discovering the grave was open Mary of Magdala ran straight for Peter the beloved disciple. Even though Peter had failed miserably he was still held in high regard by all the disciples. Peter was greatly loved by God and regardless of his many failures Peter was honored by Jesus on the cross.

John 19:25–27 reads, "Now there stood by the cross of Jesus his mother, and his mother's sister, Mary the wife of Cleophas, and Mary Magdalene. When Jesus therefore saw his mother, and the disciples standing by, whom he loved, he saith unto his mother, Woman behold thy son! Then saith he to the disciples, Behold thy mother! And from that hour that disciple took her unto his own house."

The very last words spoken by Jesus are directed at his beloved mother and disciples. Jesus' death on the cross paid for all of man's sin. From that time forward John and the disciples ensured that Jesus' mother (Mary) would be protected and that all of her needs would be met. The danger was great with the Sanhedrin and now the Roman Government was willing to execute those that are found guilty of blasphemy. Members of the

Sanhedrin were looking for all those who were associated with Jesus. Consequently, John and the Apostle went to great lengths to ensure that Jesus' mother (Mary) was protected and out of danger.

Again, we see the eminence of Peter as he is the first to witness the risen Savior.

Peter as head of the church and beloved of God was the first to see the risen Lord and Savior. Jesus' second appearance was in a locked room with the eleven disciples.

Luke 24:36–43 reads, "And as they thus spake, Jesus himself stood in the midst of them, and saith unto them, Peace be unto you. But they were terrified and affrighted, and supposed that they had seen a spirit. And he said unto them, Why are ye troubled? and why do thoughts arise in your hearts? Behold my hands and my feet, that it is I myself: handle me, and see; for a spirit hath not flesh and bones, as ye see me have. And when he had thus spoken, he showed them his hands and his feet. And while they yet believed not for joy, and wondered, he said unto them, Have ye here any meat. And they gave him a piece of a broiled fish, and of a honeycomb. And he took it, and did eat before them."

Jesus' second appearance was before his eleven disciples in a room that had been locked from the inside. In a moment Jesus appeared standing before his disciples in a body that appeared as any other with both skin and bones. In fact, He invited his disciples to examine his hands and feet to verify that it was his body that was crucified on the cross. He also ate fish and honey. This appearance by Jesus in front of his disciples gave them no room for doubt that Jesus had died and then rose from the grave. It was God's grace that allowed for the repentance and remission of sin for all of mankind. Peter and all the disciples were at this time commissioned by God to preach the saving grace of Jesus beginning with Jerusalem and then all the nations.

John 20:21–23 reads, "Then said Jesus to them again, Peace be unto you: as my Father hath sent me, even so send I you. And when he had said this, he breathed on them, and saith unto them, Receive ye the Holy Ghost: Whosoever sins ye remit, they are remitted unto them, and whosesoever sins ye retain, they are retained."

Peter and the disciples were given the Holy Spirit to continue the work of Jesus and the preaching of the good news that Jesus had risen and had defeated death for all of mankind. The disciples were now preaching that Jesus was the ultimate sacrifice or all man's sin. The church and its' people may now receive the forgiveness of their sins by believing in the death and resurrection of Jesus, God's only Son.

Peter had failed and denied he knew Jesus three times after Jesus was found guilty of blasphemy and was sentenced to death. Jesus, after His resurrection confronts Peter three times with the same question.

John 21:15-17 reads, "So when they had dined, Jesus saith to Simon Peter, Simon son of Jonah, lovest thou me more than these? He said unto him, Yea, Lord; you knowest that I love thee. He saith unto him, Feed my lambs. He said to him again the second time, Simon, son of Jonah, lovest thou me? He said unto him, Yes, Lord; thou knowest that I love thee. He saith unto him, Feed my sheep. He saith unto him the third time, Simon, son of Jonah, lovest thou me? Peter was grieved because he said unto him the third time, Lovest thou me? And he said unto him, Lord, thou knowest that I love thee. Jesus saith unto him, Feed my sheep."

Peter is confronted by Jesus asking him if he loved his Savior, Jesus. The questions by Jesus and the answers by Peter are heard by all and there is now no doubt that Peter has been confirmed and that Peter is committed to completing his mission to preach the gospel. Peter the head of the church and commissioned by God still failed and still had lapses in judgment. Peter's journey and all of mans' journeys are not without daily challenges due to the old natural man and Satan. However, God does not fail us, His grace and forgiveness is never ending and is available to all those who repent.

Jesus' challenge to Peter is that if he loves Him he needs to feed His sheep. It is not uncommon for sheep to wander while they are grazing and will at times get lost. They have no sense of direction and if they become lost they cannot find their way back to the flock. Man has no sense of spiritual direction and if he becomes lost he needs someone to help him find his way back to his Master and Lord. Sheep are completely defenseless, without sharp teeth, sharp claws, or the speed to escape an attack from a wolf or mountain lion. It is important for sheep to stay close to their shepherd for protection. The same is true for man. Man needs to stay close to God on a daily basis to be able to consume spiritual food and water to maintain enough strength to withstand the attacks from Satan and his demons.

Jesus was not only commanding Peter to feed his sheep and the church, but to maintain a close daily relationship with God that would provide the strength to withstand the relentless attacks from Satan and his demons. Man has a soul that is completely dependent on spiritual nourishment. This nourishment comes from only one source and that one source is God that transforms the soul in daily prayer and study.

Peter at this point was growing in strength and power as the Holy Spirit took on a greater role in his life. Peter's message to the people of Jerusalem had a huge impact and many believed in the message of the cross.

Acts 2:14–36 reads, "But Peter, standing up with the eleven, lifted up his voice, and said unto them, ye men of Judea, and all that dwell at Jerusalem, be this known unto you, and hearken to my words: For these are not drunken, as ye suppose, seeing it is but the third hour of the day. But this is that which was spoken by the prophet Joel; AND IT SHALL COME TO PASS IN THE LAST DAYS, SAITH GOD, I WILL POUR OUT OF MY SPIRIT UPON ALL FLESH: AND YOUR SONS AND YOUR DAUGHTERS SHALL PROPHESY, AND YOUR YOUNG MEN SHALL SEE VISIONS, AND YOUR OLD MEN SHALL DREAM DEAMS: AND ON MY SERVANTS AND ON MY HANDMAIDENS I WILL POUR OUT IN THOSE DAYS OF MY SPIRIT; AND THEY SHALL PROPHESY: AND I WILL SHOW WONDERS IN HEAVEN ABOVE, AND SIGNS IN THE EARTH BENEATH: BLOOD, AND FIRE, AND VAPOR OF SMOKE: THE SUN SHALL BE TURNED INTO DARKNESS, AND THE MOON INTO BLOOD, BEFORE THAT GREAT AND NOTABLE DAY OF THE LORD COME: AND IT SHALL COME TO PASS, THAT WHOSOEVER SHALL CALL ON THE NAME OF THE LORD SHALL BE SAVED. Ye men of Israel, hear these words; Jesus of Nazareth, a man approved of God among you by miracles and wonders and signs, which God did by him in the midst of you, as ye yourselves also know: Him, being delivered by the determinate counsel and foreknowledge of God, ye have taken, and by wicked hands have crucified and slain: Whom God hath raised up, having loosed the pains of death: because it was not possible that he should be holden of it. For David speaketh concerning him, I FORESAW THE LORD ALWAYS BEFORE MY FACE; FOR HE IS ON MY RIGHT HAND, THAT I SHOULD NOT BE MOVED: THEREFORE DID MY HEART REJOICE, AND MY TOUGUE WAS GLAD, MOREOVER ALSO MY FLESH SHALL REST IN HOPE: BECAUSE THOU WILT NOT LEAVE MY SOUL IN HELL, NEITHER WILT THOU SUFFER THINE HOLY ONE TO SEE CORRUPTION. THOU HAST MADE KNOWN TO ME THE WAYS OF LIFE; THOU SHALT MAKE ME FULL OF JOY WITH THY COUNTENANCE. Men and brethren, let me freely speak unto you of the patriarch David, that he is both dead and buried, and his sepulcher is with us unto this day. Therefore being a prophet, and knowing that God had sworn with an oath to him, that of the fruit of his loins, according to the flesh, he would raise up Christ to sit on his throne. He seeing this before spake of the resurrection of Christ, that his soul was not left in hell, neither his flesh did see corruption. This Jesus hath God raised up, whereof we all are witnesses. Therefore being by the right hand of God exalted and having received of the Father the promise of the Holy Ghost, he hath shed forth this, which ye now see and hear. For David is not ascended into the heaven: but he saith himself, THE LORD SAID UNTO MY LORD, SIT THOU ON MY RIGHT HAND, UNTIL I MAKE THY FOES THY FOOTSTOOL. Therefore let all the house of Israel know assuredly, that God hath made that same Jesus, whom ye have crucified, both Lord and Christ."

The Holy Spirit on the day of Pentecost filled Peter and caused him to deliver a message so strong that it converted over 3,000 people to the belief in Jesus Christ as the risen Savior for all of mankind. Peter spoke of the fulfillment of the prophecy that Jesus would come to be the sacrifice for all of man's sins, that his works and His resurrection would attest that He was the Messiah. He was condemned and crucified by Jewish and Roman Courts for confessing to the truth that He was the Messiah. He was ascended into heaven to sit at God's right hand and has now sent the Holy Spirit to direct and strengthen our spirits. Jesus our glorified Messiah has poured forth the Holy Spirit. We pray today for the out pouring of the Holy Spirit for the spiritual conversions of millions of people whose spirit is either consumed by self or lost to the desire of money and power.

Peter's spirit and spiritual life was growing in strength to the point of allowing the Holy Spirit to perform miracles through him.

Acts 9:39-43 reads, "Then Peter arose and went with them. When he was come, they brought him into the upper chamber: and all the widows stood by him weeping, and showing the coats and garments which Dorcas made, while she was with them. But Peter put them all forth, and kneeled down, and prayed; and turning him to the body said, Tabitha, arise. And she opened her eyes, and when she saw Peter, she sat up. And he gave her his hand, and lifted her up, and when he has called the saints and widows, presented her alive. And it was known throughout all Joppa; and many believed in the Lord. And it came to pass, that he tarried many days in Joppa with one Simon a tanner."

This first and most powerful miracle performed by an Apostle was completed by Peter. This miracle future confirmed Peter's position as leader of the Apostles. In addition, Peter spent some time in Joppa with Simon the tanner, preaching and teaching to both Jews and Gentiles.

The second miracle related to Peter was the conversion of a Gentile, a Roman centurion. Peter was then contacted by Cornelius a centurion living in Caesarea a city located north of Joppa on the Mediterranean Sea. Cornelius was visited by an angel who told him to contact Peter. So Cornelius summoned Peter to come to Caesarea.

Acts 10:25–28 reads, "And as Peter was coming in, Cornelius met him, and fell down at his feet, and worshiped him. But Peter took him up, saying, Stand up: I myself also am a man. And as he talked with him, he went in, and found many that were come together. And he said unto them, Ye know how that it is an unlawful thing for a man that is a Jew to keep company, or come unto one of another nation; but God hath showed me that I should not call any man common or unclean."

Peter again realized with God's assistance that God was no respecter of people. There is no place in Christianity for prejudice against another man regardless if he is a Gentile or Jew. God accepts all men from all nations who believe in Him, love Him, and obey Him.

Peter's words were revolutionary and moved the church into the worldwide mission of providing the saving Grace in the faith of the Lord Jesus Christ. The Holy Spirit came upon all that heard Peter's message and believed. All men are equal in God's sight. It is man's decision to either accept judgment or salvation. Salvation is faith that is based on the belief on the risen Savior, Jesus Christ, God's only Son.

As Peter's reputation began to grow, so did resentment grow among the Jews and the Romans against the church.

Acts 12:1–3 reads, "Now about that time Herod the King stretched forth his hands to vex certain of the church. And he killed James the brother of John with the sword. And because he saw it pleased the Jews, he proceeded further to take Peter also. Then were the days of unleavened bread."

King Herod was under pressure due to a famine and decided to blame the church for Israel's problems. King Agrippa 1 was aware of the Jewish resentment of the early Christian church and took advantage of every opportunity to curry favor of the Jews. In this case, the King found that it pleased the Jews when he executed James (son of Zebedee and brother of John) with a sword, so Herod imprisoned Peter. A public trial would allow all the Jews to express their hatred for the young Christian church and increase Herod's status in Jerusalem.

Witnesses to a Great Miracle

Peter was placed in chains and under heavy guard 24 hours a day.

Acts 12:7-8 reads, "And behold, the angel of the Lord came upon him, and a light shinned in the prison: and he smote Peter on the side, and raised him up, saying, Arise up quickly, And his chains fell from his hands. And the angel said unto him, Gird thyself, and bind on thy sandals. And so he did. And he saith unto him, Cast thy garment about thee, and follow me."

Even though Peter was under heavy guard and in chains, they were not enough to prevent God from freeing Peter from this prison. It was God's angel that took the chains from Peter, prevented the guards from acting, and opened the gates without keys. Peter was free from certain death and returned to the house of Mary (John Mark's house). The first response from the household was it must be Peter's angel. Peter told the household to tell James (Jesus half brother) what had transpired and that he was free. Peter left the area and began his ministry possibly to Asia Minor.

The Apostle Peter also encountered some conflict when he traveled to Antioch where he was confronted by Paul for not eating with the Gentiles.

Galatians 2:11-14 reads, "But when Peter was come to Antioch, I withstood him to the face, because he was to be blamed. For before that certain came from James, he did eat with the Gentiles: but when they were came, he withdrew and separated himself, fearing them which were of the circumcision. And the other Jews dissembled likewise with him; insomuch that Barnabas also was carried away with their dissimulation."

Again, God was patience with Peter as he tried to understand the relationship between the Jew and Gentile. Peter a Jew, was struggling with following Jewish law and at the same time did not want to offend the Gentiles and Paul a Roman by birth. Paul and the Gentiles are not bound by Jewish law and are equal to all men in God's eye.

Galatians 2:16 reads, "Knowing that a man is not justified by the works of the law, but by the faith of Jesus Christ, even we have believed in Jesus Christ, that we might be justified by the faith of Christ, and not by works of the law: for by the works of the law shall no flesh be justified."

Again, God reminds Peter that his salvation is only possible by the atoning death of his only Son. A believer in Jesus Christ lives a life that glorifies God by obeying, serving, and praising God for his countless blessings. Salvation cannot be achieved by performing goods works or by obeying the Jewish law. Salvation is only possible by believing in the death and resurrection of God's only Son, the Lord Jesus Christ.

ANALYSIS OF THE APOSTLE PETER

God loved Peter regardless of his many human frailties and failures. God took Peter a fisherman from Galilee with little formal education and built the Christian church with the Apostle. God was extremely patient with Peter even though he denied Christ three times and struggled in understanding God's direction for his life. Peter was the first Apostle to recognize Jesus as the Messiah, the first to take on the commitment to full service, and the first to lead the Apostles in forming the church. His single purpose in life was to please God, preach the gospel, serve the poor, and to lead the Apostles. The Holy Spirit over took Peter in a great way that allowed him to perform miracles, to preach a message that saved the souls of over three thousand in one meeting, and to direct the Apostles in forming the church. Peter was truly a unique individual that lived for his Savior and devoted a hundred percent to saving souls.

The Jewish culture was deeply rooted in following the Jewish leadership and obeying Jewish law. Any deviation from the Jewish law was strongly discouraged and could result in stoning. King Herod and the Roman government were constantly looking for any signs of trouble within the local Jewish community for fear of a revolt against their ruthless control. When Herod learned he would gain favor for killing James, he started an effort to punish the Apostles and jailed Peter. Herod's plan was to jail Peter and place him on display in a public trial. This would both allow the Jews to air their hatred of the Apostles and for Herod to build a good reputation among the Jews. Peter and the Apostles were forced to avoid both the Jewish and Roman leadership to prevent persecution and stay alive.

Peter traveled to Antioch (ruins lie near Antakya, Turkey) where Christianity grew in popularity. Antioch is also known as the Cradle of Christianity.

It is believed Peter then traveled to Rome where he worked in forming the early Christian church in Rome. It is believed this was also during the time of Nero and the great fire that consumed most of Rome. Emperor Nero placed the blame for the fire on the Christians in the city and looked to jail Peter and have him put to death. The Apostle Peter in 64AD elected to be crucified upside down, since he felt he was not worthy to be crucified in the same manner as Jesus his Savior.

6.

James (the Greater) the Apostle

JAMES THE APOSTLE (12 BC to 44 AD) was the son of Zebedee and Salome and older brother of John the Apostle. James was also known as James the Greater due to his age or stature and to distinguish him from Jesus' brother, James. It is also believed he was older than the other Apostles. He was the first Apostle to be martyred by a sword from King Herod Agrippa of Judaea. As a member of the inner circle of Jesus the Apostle had witnessed the raising of Jairus' daughter, the Transfiguration of Jesus, and Jesus' agony in the Garden of Gethsemane.

James was known as the "Son of Thunder" because of his enthusiasm, his energy, fiery temper, and his willingness to tackle any issue. This out spoken demeanor may have caught the attention of the Jewish and Roman leadership resulting in his capture and execution.

James' father (Zebedee) was a fisherman on the Sea of Galilee and seemed to be successful in this business with some employees. They probably lived in Bethsaida or Capernaum on the Sea of Galilee. Salome his mother became a follower of Jesus and ministered unto Jesus at times.

Mark 1:19–20 reads, "And when he had gone a little farther thence, he saw James the son of Zebedee, and John his brother, who also were in the ship mending their nets. And straightway he called them: and they left their father Zebedee in the ship with the hired servants, and went after him."

Jesus' summons to James and John was one for a lifetime of commitment to preaching and teaching the gospel of Christ. Obviously, the two men were ready to make this decision without reservation. There was no discussion, no difficulties, they knew and recognized the divine will of Jesus

James (the Greater) the Apostle

as the Christ. It is believed they knew of Jesus and had already determined Jesus was the Savior that was prophesied.

There is little information about James' preaching of the gospel after Christ' ascension. It is believed he preached to all twelve tribes of the Jews and made mission trips to Spain. James was present at Peter's home when Jesus cured Peter's mother-in-law. James was also present when Jesus raised Jairus' daughter from the dead.

Paul did express his intention to visit Spain and to minister unto all Gentiles to the limits of the West. He would also avoid building upon another's foundation.

Romans 15:24 reads, "Whensoever I take my journey into Spain, I will come to you: for I trust to see you in my journey, and to be brought on my way thitherward by you, if first I be somewhat filled with your company."

This verse acknowledges Paul's intentions to visit Spain, but makes no mention of James and his work in Spain. Other historical documentation and Church history provide more information.

On one occasion, Salome (mother of James and John) came to Jesus and asked that her sons sit at the right and left of Him in heaven.

Matthew 20:20–23 reads, "Then came to him the mother of Zebedee's children with her sons, worshiping him , and desiring a certain thing of him. And he said unto her, What wilt thou? She said unto him. Grant that these my two sons may sit, the one on thy right hand, and the other on the left, in thy kingdom. But Jesus answered and said, Ye know not what ye ask. Are ye able to drink of the cup that I shall drink of, and to be baptized with the baptism that I am baptized with? They say unto him, We are able. And he saith unto them, Ye shall drink indeed of my cup, and be baptized with the baptism that I am baptized with: but to sit on my right, and on my left, is not mine to give, but it shall be given to them for whom it is prepared of my Father."

Salome and her sons clearly understood that Jesus' life was going to end and that there was a heaven and they were willing to suffer and die as Jesus. Salome as a loving mother of two wanted the best for her sons. Salome continued to care for Jesus and her sons as they continued to preach the way to salvation, healed those who were in need, and provide for the poor. Some believe that the mother of Jesus and Salome were sisters.

Jesus was asking James and John if they were ready to share the cup that represents the death and suffering of Jesus. They both answered that they were willing to accept the cup. James' martyrdom came a few years later in 44 AD. He was the first to be honored to follow his Master and Lord in being martyred.

The site of martyrdom is located in the Armenian Apostolic Cathedral of St. James in Jerusalem where King Agrippa's ordered his beheading. It is believed that the Apostle James preached both in Israel and in Iberia, Spain. The Apostle James martyrdom and tomb is also located at the Cathedral of Santiago de Compostela, Spain.

ANALYSIS OF THE APOSTLE JAMES

Jesus loved The Apostle James and The Apostle John and called the brothers, "Sons of Thunder."

The Apostle James was the older brother of the Apostle John and lived in area of Capernaum and Bethsaida. As a son of Zebedee he was a fisherman in the family business. It is believed he had a fiery temper that could be aroused if provoked. He had no patience with those that did not believe and in one case wanted Jesus to destroy an entire Samaritan village for not welcoming them. He did a lot of preaching and became effective at delivering a message that challenged the Jewish leadership.

As the other disciples, James spent a great deal of time with Jesus learning and grasping the true meaning of Jesus' teachings. By the end of Jesus' teachings James had a superior understanding and became a master at presenting the message to all of mankind. The Apostle John and James were brothers of like mind and cared for each other deeply. The unforeseen and shocking execution of the Apostle James was especially traumatic to his younger brother the Apostle John.

This execution represents a turning point as the Roman Government learns that the killing of Christians would bring the admiration of the Jewish leadership. From that point the persecution of Christians was encouraged since it worked to improve the relationship between the Jewish community and the Roman Government.

The Apostle James was extremely courageous and bold and willing to stand in front of any leadership whether Jewish or Roman and proclaim the message of salvation for all of mankind. When Jesus asked if they would drink the cup, the Apostles said yes knowing that they may lose their lives.

7.

John the Apostle

JOHN THE APOSTLE (6 AD to 100 AD) was one of first apostles to be recruited by Jesus for ministry. He was the son of Zebedee and Salome. His father Zebedee had a fishing business that included John, his brother James and a number of employees. It is believed he was the author of the Gospel of John, the three Epistles of John, and the book of Revelation. According to the book of Mark, John is always mentioned after James and is considered the younger son.

John states the purpose of the book in John 20:31, which reads, "But these are written, that ye might believe that Jesus is the Christ, the son of God; and that believing ye might have life through his name." John defines the gospel clearly as either living in the light or living in the darkness. He also explains that those that are living in the darkness hate the light because it exposes their evil deeds, their evil desires, and their evil priorities.

Mark 3:17 reads, "And James the son of Zebedee, and John the brother of James; and he surnamed them Boanerges, which is, The Sons of Thunder:"

Jesus named the brothers the "Sons of Thunder" for good reason. They were both fearless in their approach to preaching that Jesus was the Messiah to the twelve tribes of Israel. They were outspoken, used words that were emotionally charged for the Jews and confronted those that believed that following the law was all that was required to spend eternity in heaven.

Luke 9:53–55 reads, "And they did not receive him, because his face was as though he would go to Jerusalem. And when his disciples James and John saw this, they said, Lord, wilt thou that we command fire to come down from heaven, and consume them, even as Elijah did? But he turned, and rebuked them, and said, Ye know not what manner of spirit ye are of.

For the Son of man is not come to destroy man's lives, but to save them. And they went to another village."

The brothers at this time identify themselves with Elijah and the time when fire came from heaven to destroy the entire altar and sacrifice. The brothers had little patience with the Samaritans and were enraged that this village did not welcome Jesus. They wanted the wrath of God to destroy the entire village and its people. These were not men that would understand or appreciate what is transpiring in some churches today. The "feel good" church of today makes it easy to be a Christian since nothing is taught about sin and repentance. Sin is not defined and people are lead to believe they can continue living a life that is consumed in striving for more wealth, for more material possessions, and for some higher status in the community. You see no love in their lives, no peace, and no love for others. Their focus is entirely on themselves and what they can gain or steal from others. They are like leaches on society that have no purpose other than to suck the life out of others.

In many cases, today's church has turned into a entertainment community center where the wages of sin is not mentioned and people have no understanding of the message presented by the Apostle John and the Apostle James.

1 John 3:7 reads, "Little children, let no man deceive you: he that doeth righteousness is righteous, even as he is righteous."

Sin is of Satan and has no place in the church. The church in many situations no longer teaches about what is the real purpose of life and what is required of man on a daily basis. Jesus and disciples were persecuted and martyred because they spoke of sin and challenged the Jews to accept Jesus as their Messiah.

Matthew 7:13 reads, "Enter ye in at the strait gate: for wide is the gate, and broad is the way, that leadeth to destruction, and many there be, which go in thereat. Because strait is the gate, and narrow is the way, which leadeth unto life, and few there be that find it."

The gate to eternal life is narrow and Jesus is the gate that one must pass through to find God's grace and salvation.

Jesus corrected the Apostle John and the Apostle James and told them that he would not destroy the village because he came to save lives and not to destroy them. Jesus again showed his love and patience for the Samaritans and allowed them more time to make a decision of commitment to Christianity.

John the Apostle

The Beloved Disciple, the disciple whom Jesus loved is believed to be John the Evangelist. He is referred to in a number of verses:

John 13:23-26 reads, "Now there was leaning on Jesus bosom one of his disciples, whom Jesus loved. Simon Peter therefore beckoned to him, that he should ask who it should be of whom he spake. He then lying on Jesus breast saith unto him, Lord, who is it? Jesus answered, He it is, to whom I shall give a sop, when I have dipped it. And when he had dipped the sop, he gave it to Judas Iscariot, the son of Simon."

Jesus knew that His time was growing short and during the last supper He began to prepare the disciples for the betrayal, arrest, death and resurrection.

It was John the Evangelist that was seated next to Jesus and it was John who heard Jesus say who it was who betrayed Him. John was part of the inner circle of disciples that Jesus trusted and loved. In this situation, Jesus confided only in John because he knew that some of the other disciples could strike out in anger. For example, Peter was emotional, carried a sword and could act impetuously.

Even though Jesus was going through the anguish of dying on the cross he still was concerned about His mother and the Apostle John.

John 19:26-27 reads, "When Jesus therefore saw his mother, and the disciple standing by, whom he loved, he saith unto his mother, Woman, behold they son! Then saith he to the disciple, Behold thy mother! And from that hour that disciple took her unto his own home."

It is Apostle John who records these words and it is John who accepts the responsibility for the care of Jesus' mother, Mary. Jesus tells his mother that John is now her son and John will now care for her. Jesus then tells John that Mary is his mother and he is now responsible for her care. No greater honor could be given to a disciple then the care for Jesus mother, Mary. Without a doubt Jesus held a special place in his heart for John to entrust the care of His mother to him.

It was the Apostle John and the Apostle Peter that first heard the news of Jesus' resurrection from Mary Magdalene.

John 20:1-4 reads, "The first day of the week cometh Mary Magdalene early, when it was yet dark, unto the sepulcher, and seeth the stone taken away from the sepulcher. Then she runneth, and cometh to Simon Peter, and to the other disciple, whom Jesus loved, and saith unto them, They have taken away the Lord out of the sepulcher, and we know not where they have laid him. Peter therefore went forth, and the other disciple, and came to the sepulcher. So they ran both together: and the other disciple did outrun Peter, and came first to the sepulcher."

It was Apostle John who out ran the Apostle Peter to the sepulcher to see the empty tomb.

When Jesus appeared to the disciples who were fishing on the Sea of Galilee it was John who first recognized that it was the Lord standing on the shore.

John 21:5–7 reads, "Then Jesus saith unto them, children have ye any meat? They answered him, No. And he saith unto them, Cast the net on the right side of the ship, and ye shall find. They cast therefore, and now they were not able to draw it for the multitude of fishes. Therefore that disciple whom Jesus loved saith unto Peter, It is the Lord. Now when Simon Peter heard that it was the Lord, he girt his fisher's coat unto him, for he was naked, and did cast himself into the sea."

The Apostle John is involved in the miracle of catching so many fish that it almost sinks the ships. In fact, the Apostle John appears to be involved in most of Jesus' miracles.

The Apostle Peter at one point asked a question about the Apostle John and his future. Jesus basically tells Apostle Peter that it is not any of his concern and that he should concentrate on following Jesus' direction.

John 21:20–23 reads, "Then Peter, turning about, seeth the disciple whom Jesus loved following; which also leaned on his bread at supper, and said, Lord, which is he that betrayeth thee? Peter seeing him saith to Jesus, Lord, and what shall this man do? Jesus saith unto him, "If I will that he tarry till I come, what is that to thee? Follow thou me."

Jesus at this point gives some indication that he may have special plans for the Apostle John and his future mission. The Apostle John did live out his life to the age of 94 at the Church of Ephesus where he continued his work preaching and writing.

The Apostle John confirms that he can testify of these facts since he was physically present with Jesus as he preached, healed the weak and died on the cross to provide all of mankind a path to salvation.

John 21:24 reads, "This is the disciple which testifieth of these things, and wrote these things: and we know that his testimony is true."

The Holy Bible only records a small portion of all that was spoken by Jesus and the many acts of passion He completed. The Apostle John guided by the Holy Spirit recorded all that needed to be transcribed and to be included in the Holy Bible.

John the Apostle

The Apostle John was part of the inner circle of Disciples that received personal instruction from Jesus as he raised people from the dead, healed people from many different illnesses and provided the way of salvation.

Mark 5:37–40 reads, "And he suffered no man to follow him, save Peter, and James, and John the brother of James. And he cometh to the house of the ruler of the synagogue, and seeth the tumult, and them that wept and wailed greatly. And when he was come in, he saith unto them, Why make ye this ado, and weep? The damsel is not dead, but sleepeth. And they laughed him to scorn. But when he had put them all out, he taketh the father and the mother of the damsel, and them that were with him, and entereth in where the damsel was lying."

Jesus instructs John, Peter, and James that those that are disruptive, negative, and faithless need to be removed from the area. Jesus at this time purged the room, the house, and the premises of all the people that were laughing him to scorn. Our thoughts, deeds, and emotions are either righteous or sinful. People are either in the light or in the darkness. In this case, sin and Satan were in control of these people that were laughing. Each day we need to be aware of our speech, thoughts, and emotions to ensure they are not sinful.

Jesus was teaching the Apostle John and others you should not proceed until the area is clean of sin and those that are present are believers. This powerful and miraculous miracle occurred when Jesus was in complete control. We struggle with righteousness and sin throughout the day as we entertain ideas and thoughts, consider actions to take, and decide on language to use.

John was also present in the Upper Room and in the Garden of Gethsemane. It was late when the disciples left the last supper and walked through the dark streets of Jerusalem on their way to the Mount of Olives. The Apostle John had no idea that the information he just received about the betrayal from Jesus would transpire within hours at the Garden of Gethsemane. Jesus continued to teach and prepare his disciples about His betrayal, death and resurrection.

John 15:1–7 reads, "I am the true vine, and my Father is the husbandman. Every branch in me that beareth not fruit he taketh away; and every branch that beareth fruit, he purgeth it, that it may bring forth more fruit. Now ye are clean through the word which I have spoken unto you. Abide in me, and I in you. As the branch cannot bear fruit of itself, except it abide in the vine: no more can ye, except ye abide in me. I am the vine, ye are the branches: He that abideth in me, and I in him, the same bringeth forth much fruit: for without me ye can do nothing. If a man abide not in me, he is cast forth as a branch, and is withered; and men gather them, and cast them into fire, and they are burned. If ye abide in me, and my words abide in you, ye shall ask what ye will, and it shall be done unto you."

Jesus explains to the Apostle John and to the other disciples that they were to preach the gospel and to allow the Holy Spirit to save souls. He also explains that as their understanding becomes more complete and their testimony becomes more effective He would become more involved in their lives. Jesus their Lord through the Holy Spirit guided them, he corrected them, and he open new paths for them to follow.

Jesus continued to instruct his disciples and to ensure them that he would provide for their needs. They would need to allow the Holy Spirit to take control of their lives and direct them so that many may hear God's word and believe.

The Apostle John and the other disciples continued to walk in the dark to the Garden of Gethsemane where Jesus prayed. It was the Apostle John who listened with great care to record Jesus' prayer.

John 17:1–26 reads. "These words spake Jesus, and lifted up his eyes to heaven, and said, Father, the hour is come; glorify thy Son, that the Son also may glorify thee. As thou hast given him power over all flesh, that he should give eternal life to as many as thou hast given him. And this is life eternal, that they might know thee the only true God, and Jesus Christ, whom thou hast sent. I have glorified thee on the earth: I have finished the work which thou gavest me to do. And now, O Father, glorify thou me with thine own self with the glory which I had with thee before the world was. I have manifested thy name unto the men which thou gavest me out of the world: thine they were, and thou gavest them me: and they have kept thy word. Now they have know that all things whatsoever thou hast given me are of thee. For I have given unto them the words which thou gavest me; and they have received them, and have known surely that I came out from thee, and they have believed that thou didst send me. I pray for them: I pray not for the world, but for them which thou hast given me; for they are thine. And all mine are thine, and thine are mine; and I am glorified in them. And now I am no more in the world, but these are in the world, and I come to thee. Holy Father, keep through thine own name those whom thou hast given me, that they may be one, as we are. While I was with them in the world, I kept them in thy name: those that thou gavest me I have kept, and none of them is lost, but the son of perdition; that the scripture might be fulfilled. And now come I to thee; and these things I speak to the world, that they might have my joy fulfilled in themselves. I have given them thy word; and the world hath hated them, because they are not of the world, even as I am not of the world. I pray not that thou shouldest take them out of the world, but that shouldest keep them from evil. They are not of the world, even as I am not of the world. Sanctity them through thy truth; thy word is truth. As thou hast sent me into the world, even so have I also sent them into the world. And for their sakes I sanctify myself, that they also might be sanctified through the truth. Neither pray I for these alone, but for them also which shall believe on me through their word: That they all may be one; as thou, Father, art in me, and I in thee, that they also may be one in us: that the world may believe that thou hast sent me. And the glory which thou gavest me I have given them; that they may be one, even as we are one: I in them, and thou in me, that they may be made perfect in one; and that the world may know that thou hast sent me, and hast loved them, as thou hast loved me. Father, I will that they also, whom thou hast given me, be with me where I am; that they may behold my glory, which thou hast given me: for thou lovedst, me before the foundation of the world. O righteous Father, the world hath not know thee: but I have know thee, and these have know that thou hast sent me. And I have declared unto them thy name, and will declare it: that the love wherewith thou hast loved me may be in them, and I in them."

The Apostle John was there in the Garden of Gethsemane with Jesus when He prayed and recorded His words. Jesus' prayer was to glorify God, and to benefit those present (his disciples) and for future generations. Jesus prayed that his work is complete here on earth and that He is resting in God's will and His return to the realm of eternity.

Jesus also prays for the disciples and their faith, knowledge, love, and the indwelling of the Holy Spirit. As the Son, he verifies that His disciples are no longer part of the world that hates them because of their faith in their Lord Jesus the Christ. He prays for those that will become believers by hearing the words spoken by His disciples.

The prayer is also a request from the Son to the Father for glory to be given out so that all that hear and see may be blessed. This glory is based on the manifestation of God's gracious love of the Father for the Son and for all of mankind.

The Son was glorified by the Father by giving him authority over all of man's weaknesses. The Son glorified the Father by giving eternal life to all those who believed in the Lord Jesus Christ.

The Apostle John and his understanding of the glorification of the Father and the Son were based on this prayer, Jesus' life, and teachings. The relationship that was lost with the fall of man will be restored due the works completed by Jesus, His obedience, death, and resurrection.

It is believed that the Apostle John continued to live in Jerusalem for a number of years even after the Crucifixion and Resurrection of Jesus. In about 36 AD, the persecution of Christians continued with Stephen being stoned to death for preaching the gospel. The persecution continued as when the Apostle James was executed in about 44AD by King Agrippa. The Apostle John experienced a great loss with the death of his brother James and now the danger was too great for his family to live in the Promised Land settled by the twelve tribes of Judah. John rose to a position of prominence in the Christian Church and was able to move before the destruction of Jerusalem in 70AD by the Romans.

Sometime after this continued persecution of Christians the Apostles started moving to others areas outside of Israel. At this time it is believed the Apostle John moved his family (including the Mother of Jesus) to Ephesus of Asia (Turkey). He was able to move his family away from immediate danger and help spread the gospel to the West. The Apostle John continued his preaching for a number of years and worked with the Apostle Paul, the Apostle Peter, the Apostle Timothy and others in spreading the gospel throughout Asia and West to Europe. Ephesus was known as a city of learning where Christians such as the Apostle John and the Apostle Paul were able to preach the gospel to crowds gathered in the lecture halls. The ministry grew as more people witnesses the healing power of the Holy Spirit and those that were released from demons.

Ephesus was the capital of Asia Minor and the center for trade in the area. The temple of Artemis was built in Ephesus by the Greeks and attracted many worshipers from all around the area. With the worshipers of pagan gods came a great deal of money for the city of Ephesus. There were seven Christian churches in the area that Paul and John ministered to. Like Antioch and Cornith, Ephesus was a port city that allowed many of the disciples to travel between churches. It is believed that the Apostle Paul wrote many of his letters here over a period as long as three years and may have also been imprisoned in Ephesus.

Emperor Domitian realized that these worshipers of the goddess Artemis were responsible for donating a great deal of money to the Roman Government and that the new Christian Churches were preventing more donations. The Roman Government generally considered the Christian church another cult that caused problems for the government by challenging the worship of pagan gods and the beliefs of other religions.

The Roman Government had increased its efforts to eliminate the Christian church by capturing its leaders and placing them in prison or charging them with some type of punishment such as banishment. The Apostle John was arrested and banished to the small island of Patmos. These small islands did have mines where criminals were forced to work under extreme conditions.

As a "Son of Thunder," the Apostle John had experienced a great deal of joy and sorrow. While imprisoned on the Island of Patmos the Apostle John began to be given great insights by the Holy Spirit. He was able to record these ideas and visions that would be later become the book of Revelation. The Apostle John also had students, Polycarp and others that studied under his directions.

It is believed that the Apostle John was eventually released from Patmos and returned to Ephesus as head of the Church of Ephesus. The Apostle John was the last of the Apostles and died in Ephesus at an age greater than 90.

ANALYSIS OF THE APOSTLE JOHN

The Apostle John had a long and fruitful life that reached great heights of joy and great depths of despair. He had rejoiced with thousands when they made their decisions to believe that Jesus Christ was the Messiah. He had seen thousands realize they no longer needed to carry the weight of sin since God paid the price with the sacrifice of His only Son Jesus.

He was identified as John the Evangelist and was called the "Beloved Disciple" by Jesus. It is believed that it was the Apostle John who stood next to Mary when Jesus hung on the cross and it was the Apostle John that cared for Mary as his mother from that time forward. It was John who Jesus confided in during the last supper and spoke of his betrayer. John understood the message of loving your neighbor and treating others as you wish to be treated.

Witnesses to a Great Miracle

The Apostle John was a faithful student of Jesus and spent most of his adult life preaching to those who were lost to their own sense of self, recording the life of Jesus, and explaining man's relationship to his Father in heaven. John was practical in his approach to teaching the gospel and spent a great deal of time explaining the dangers that face all of mankind. He warned of false teachers and encouraged believers to be obedient to God's commands.

In the book of Revelation, the Apostle John speaks of the conflict between God and Satan and the prevailing victory by God. The Apostle John's writings were directed at the churches in Ephesus and to encourage those that were being persecuted. The Roman Empire and its leaders had destroyed Jerusalem and killed thousands of Jews and were continuing to execute Christians when it was in their best interest.

The Apostle John encouraged the Christian church and it's believes to hold fast to their belief and faith in their Lord and Savior. The persecution of Christians will continue as long as Satan is able to control and influence men's hearts and minds.

8.

The Transfiguration of Jesus

THE TRANSFIGURATION OF JESUS is one of the major miracles that occurred in the life of Jesus our Lord. As in the baptism of Jesus, God speaks directly to man and identifies Jesus as His Son.

Mark 9:7 reads, "And there was a cloud that overshadowed them: and a voice came out of the cloud, saying, This is my beloved Son: hear him." God was speaking directly to the Apostle Peter, the Apostle James, and the Apostle John that Jesus is God's Son and that Jesus is God's representative on earth.

At this point in time, Jesus was transfigured to His natural state as a glorified deity. The Apostles were allowed to be present to grow in understanding and appreciation of their Lord and Savior Jesus the Christ.

Mark 9:3 reads, "And his raiment became shinning, exceeding white as snow; so as no fuller on earth can white them."

This image of Jesus was seared into their memories and served as a constant reminder throughout the Apostles' lives of the magnitude and grandeur of God's only Son the Lord Jesus. Jesus selected the Apostle Peter, the Apostle James, and the Apostle John to experience the Transfiguration.

The apostles also witnessed the appearance of Moses and Elijah during Jesus' Transfiguration. Moses represented the law and how the law and commandments were in place to accept God's grace. Elijah represented the Prophets, the worship of God, and how God's prophesies will be fulfilled in God's grace. The Apostles were being instructed as to how Jesus' glorified body appears and how it will appear after the crucifixion and resurrection. Jesus glorified body will be able to past through walls, consumes normal food, and still appear as a natural body to the Apostles. Jesus'

Transfiguration was God's method for preparing, Moses, Elijah, and the inner circle of Apostles for the crucifixion and resurrection and to ultimately bring glory to his Son.

WITNESSES TO THE TRANSFIGURATION

Jesus selected Moses, Elijah, Peter, James, and John to be the witnesses to the Transfiguration. These five great men were able to accomplish monumental achievements in their individual lives and were an integral part of God's plans. These five men had a common tie and that tie was their complete dependence on God for their strength and direction.

MOSES AS JESUS' WITNESS

Moses like the other four witnesses started his life from a very humble beginning. Moses as a baby was found abandoned floating on the Nile River by a daughter of the Egyptian Pharaoh. He was adopted by the Pharaoh's daughter and spent his childhood in the Pharaoh's household where he was treated as a prince. Moses was aware of his Jewish heritage and had a great love and sympathy for the Jewish slaves. Moses as a young, angry, and confused man torn between two cultures had an uncontrollable temper that caused him to kill one of the Pharaohs' guards for beating a Jewish slave. Once he realized what he had done, he buried the body to buy time and started running for his life. Moses finally ended up as a sheepherder working for his father-in-law (Priest) when God spoke to him out of a burning bush. Moses had many reasons why he shouldn't follow God's direction and continued to question God's plan for his life. He was slow of speech and had difficulty in expressing his ideas. He had spent 40 years in the wilderness trying to forget his childhood as an Egyptian and the killing one of Pharaoh's guards.

At this point, Moses' self worth was nonexistent and it was only God's love that was going to carry him back to Egypt to confront the Pharaoh. God does not look at the human frailties but at a man's heart and soul to determine how they will fit into his plan.

1 Samuel 16:7 reads, "But the Lord said unto Samuel, Look not on his countenance, or on the height of his stature; because I have refused him: for the Lord seeth not as man seeth; for man looketh on the outward appearance, but the Lord looketh on the heart."

The Transfiguration of Jesus

What the world considers to be successful and desirable is not what God considers to be of value. God is interested in the heart, the soul, and the mind that is focused on God's will, direction, and plan for our lives. Moses was living in fear of what might happen if the authorities discovered what he had done. Fear is not something we are born with but is something we learn over time. Unfortunately, the mind does not determine how much fear is appropriate and many people are mislead into making the wrong decision. God worked with Moses to get him to focus less on self and fear and of what may happen and more on God's plan and what He wanted to be accomplished for the Jewish people.

Psalm 139:13-14 reads, "For thou hast possessed my reins: thou hast covered me in my mother's womb. I will praise thee: for I am fearfully and wonderfully made: marvelous are thy works; and my soul knoweth right well."

We are God's creation and we were made with His knowledge, in His presence, and with His power. We are in awe and wonder as to how He knows each one of us and how we fit in His plan. As Moses gained a better understanding of God's attributes he found a greater desire to obey and praise His creator. The natural process is that courage increases as self-worth increases.

With the blessings of God, Moses was a man that had the courage of 100 men. Moses obeyed God regardless of the risks and dangers and the fact that his death was possible at any time. He stood fast for what was morally right, the release of the Israelites.

Exodus 3:7-10 reads, "And the Lord said, I have surely seen the affliction of my people, which are in Egypt, and have heard their cry by reason of their taskmasters; for I know their sorrows. And I am come down to deliver them out of the hand of the Egyptians, and to bring them up out of that land unto a good land and a large, unto a land flowing with milk and honey; unto the place of the Canaanites, and the Hittites, and the Amorites, and the Perizzites, and the Hivites, and the Jebusites. Now therefore, behold, the cry of the children of Israel is come unto me: and I have also seen the oppression wherewith the Egyptians oppress them. Come now therefore, and I will send thee unto Pharaoh, that thou mayest bring forth my people the children of Israel out of Egypt."

God is talking directly to Moses and telling him of his concern for the Israelites. It is God's plan to take them out of Egypt and place them in a new land full of new opportunities. God also tells Moses of the imposing danger of how Pharaoh will resist the release of the Israelites and that God's mighty hand will prevail.

God was patient with Moses and spoke to Moses' brother Aaron about traveling with Moses back to Egypt to confront the Pharaoh about the release of the Jewish slaves. God had a plan not only for Moses and the Israelites, but he had a plan for the Pharaoh and the Egyptian people. God hardened the heart of the Pharaoh that prevented him from stopping the plagues, which resulted in the discrediting of his authority as a deity.

God gave Moses great courage to stand in front of the Pharaoh and to demand the release of the Israelites. The Pharaoh could have taken his life at any time without cause. God was with Moses each time he stood there demanding the release of his people and God prevented the Pharaoh from taking his life.

God has a plan for each one of us that may require us to grow and to accept new responsibilities. God may ask you to do something that may make you uncomfortable. John 2:5 reads, "His mother saith unto the servants, Whatever he saith unto you, do it."

Moses was prepared by God for the Pharaoh and knew that the Pharaoh would resist any idea for the release of the Israelites. We too are to be prepared to encounter resistance and opposition from many different directions. Acts 20:30 reads, "Also of your own selves shall men arise, speaking perverse things, to draw away disciples after them." We need to be aware of false teachers that will draw away people from the flock. Some will promise riches and wealth, but only faith accompanied by obedience to his word will receive His grace.

As Moses, we are a light to the world and we need to lead people out of their sin stained lives. John 15:18–19 reads, "If the world hate you, ye know that it hated me before it hated you. If ye were of the world, the world would love his own: but because ye are not of the world, but I have chosen you out of the world, therefore the world hateth you." Moses strong faith in God allowed him the freedom to proclaim victory over Satan and the Pharaoh.

We are to place on the armor of God. Ephesians 6:10–20 reads, "Finally, my brethren, be strong in the Lord, and in the power of his might. Put on the whole armor of God, that ye may be able to stand against the wiles of the devil. For we wrestle not against flesh and blood, but against principalities, against powers, against the rules of the darkness of this world, against spiritual wickedness in high places. Wherefore take unto you the whole armor of God, that ye may be able to withstand in the evil day, and

The Transfiguration of Jesus

having done all, to stand. Stand therefore, having your loins girt about with truth, and having on the breastplate of righteousness. And your feet shod with the preparation of the gospel of peace; Above all, Taking the shield of faith, wherewith ye shall be able to quench all the fiery darts of the wicked. And take the helmet of salvation, and the sword of the Spirit, which is the word of God: Praying always with all prayer and supplication in the Spirit, and watching thereunto with all perseverance and supplication of all saints. And for me, that utterance may be given unto me, that I may open my mouth boldly , to make know the mystery of the gospel, For which I am an ambassador in bonds; that therein I may speak boldly, as I ought to speak."

Moses lived a righteous life. He read and studied the scriptures, he knew God's truth, lived a holy, obedient, and moral life. God placed His hand on Moses and gave him great peace and courage as he confronted the Pharaoh with many plagues and the constant demand for the release of God's people.

We are to follow Moses' example as a warrior for God as we place on the armor of righteousness and stand before those that are consumed by their own greed, pride, and sense of self worth. We are to take up the shield of faith with the word of God and pray in the spirit for all of God's warriors as they confront the Pharaohs of today as they try to impose their sense of morality.

Moses was a man of God. He was blessed of God with great courage and strength to confront the Pharaoh and his army. He was a great leader that led over 600,000 Israelites for 40 years in the wildness. The contribution Moses made to God's people was monumental and allowed them to prosper and grow in a land that offered them a future. We too have an opportunity to lead people that will offer them a future.

Moses was also given the honor as God's messenger, when he received on Mount Sinai two stone tablets from God that contained the 10 commandments. God had been revealing his commandments from the beginning to man and defining sin for man. Genesis 26:5 reads, "Because that Abraham obeyed my voice, and kept my charge, my commandments, my statutes, and my laws." Since Abraham the first two commandments have been important. Exodus 20:3–5 reads, "Thou shalt have no other gods before me. Thou shalt not make unto thee any graven image, or any likeness of any thing that is in heaven above, or that is in the earth beneath, or that is in the water under the earth. Thou shalt not bow down thyself to them, nor serve them: for I the Lord thy God am a jealous God, visiting the iniquity of the fathers upon the children unto the third and fourth generation of them that hate me."

The message delivered through Moses as a reminder to the Israelites was clear and is clear today. It is extremely important that we do not worship and bow down to any other gods or deities. Mythology and the worship of gods were very popular and supported by many kings throughout the Mediterranean area. Many of the kings were corrupt and used people's superstitions and these gods to generate a great deal of money.

There are many false or pagan gods (i.e., Baal, Diana, Zeus, and Mercury) that are mentioned in the Bible. Many of the statutes of pagan gods have been destroyed, but man still continues to worship many false gods. Many of the pagan gods of the past (e.g. pleasure) have grown into many of today's billion dollar industries. Many of today's industries use the same methods to generate money as the corrupt Kings mentioned in the Bible. The promises that were made to those who made sacrifices to the pagan gods were wealth, pleasure, and a good life. The same promises are made today as companies promise pleasure, wealth, and status if money is paid for their services and products. The result has been children killing children for $500 dollar tennis shoes. The pagan gods of today are those desires and things that take priority over worshiping God. The sin of idolatry is shared by all man regardless of wealth, education, or status in the community. All men are affected and subject to the sin of worshiping false gods. There are many types of pagan gods today. For example, a person may not have time to worship God because they have devoted their entire life to fashion and spend a great amount of money trying to impress others. Others do not worship God because they are consumed by sports and other pleasures and will spend a great amount of money on tickets, and other sports related items. There are many pagan idols today that prevent man from worshiping God.

In many cases the only way to break the hold of pagan pleasures is to pray for God's strength and blessings. You can allow your relationship to grow with God by opening your heart and letting Him in your daily life. You can talk to Him about every need by opening the Bible and begin to study His Word.

Moses was painfully aware of the worship of pagan gods. After returning from Mount Sinai he discovered the Israelites had built a golden calf that they were worshiping. God's punishment was severe, but Moses continued to worship God and continued to lead the Israelites.

The Transfiguration of Jesus

ELIJAH AS JESUS' WITNESS

Elijah was also one of the few that was selected to be a witness to the Transfiguration of Jesus. Elijah was the premiere prophet and like Moses with God's strength had the courage of 100 men. He stood in front of King Ahab and his queen (Jezebel) and demanded that God be worshiped rather than Baal. He prophesied to King Ahab that the country would experience a drought that would last three years. When Ahab realized that the Elijah was correct he became enraged and sent out his men to kill him.

Elijah was a man that was completely devoted to God and spent most of his life in prayer and seeking God's will and direction. God honored Elijah and protected him in many ways. God hid Elijah, and provided him water and food that was delivered by ravens. God prevented Ahab and Jezebel from finding him regardless of the money and time spent to kill him.

Like Moses, Elijah was a great man of God that was used by God to make a major contribution in showing God's love for His people. God's people were caught in a endless circle of being forced to worship pagan gods. Many of these people were poor and were forced to make sacrifices that they could not afford.

Elijah was also greatly used by God when a contest was established with the pagan god Baal and his 450 prophets on Mount Carmel. Elijah with God's power was able to show that Baal was powerless when compared to the God of Israel.

1 King 18:22 reads. "Then said Elijah unto the people, I, even I only, remain a prophet of the Lord; but Baal's prophets are four hundred and fifty men."

At the end of the day, Elijah prayed for God to send fire to consume the altar and sacrifice. God heard Elijah's prayer and in a moment thousands of people witnessed a fire sent from heaven that consumed the entire altar, sacrifice, water, and all the stones. The 450 prophets of Baal were also destroyed. This resulted in turning the hearts of the Israelites and realizing their need to worship the God of Israel. Elijah exposed the deception of King Ahab and the pagan god Baal.

The pagan gods of today are wealth, pride, and pleasure. Today peoples' hearts and minds are consumed in the hunt for pleasure and wealth. They have no interest in learning about God and His plan for their lives.

Luke 1:16-17 reads, "And many of the children of Israel shall he turn to the Lord their God. And he shall go before him in the spirit and power of

Elijah. To turn the hearts of the fathers to the children, and the disobedient to the wisdom of the just; to make ready a people prepared for the Lord."

Elijah with God's direction was instrumental in the transformation of the people of Israel to the worship the God of Israel and created an introduction to the unfolding of the good news of the New Testament.

God will not take pleasure in destroying the wicked of the world.

Elijah was one of the most important prophets in the Bible. He was a great man of courage, obedience and a faithful servant in carrying out God's plan for the people of Israel and all of mankind. His message for the people to return to the true God is timeless and is just as important today.

The world today still has Ahab-like and Jezebel-like rulers who are corrupt and prey on the poor and weak. They look harmless from the outside, but their souls are void of any remorse or compassion for those in need. Their lives are centered on themselves and their possessions and they live for the sole purpose of gaining more to fill a need for greed. Greed like the other basic sins of the fallen man (lust, pride, envy, wrath, gluttony) are all bottomless pits without mercy. It is only the saving grace of Jesus and our Lord God that provides an answer to Satan and his demons that attack man on a daily basis.

JAMES AS JESUS' WITNESS

The Apostle James (James the Greater) was another one chosen by Jesus to be a witness to Jesus' Transfiguration. Jesus referred to James and John as the sons of thunder for their strong character and at times their quick temper. James was the older brother of John and took that responsibility with great importance. It is believed that James did spend years in Spain preaching the gospel. He knew Jesus and knew He was who He said He was. Soon after the ascension of The Lord Jesus Christ, James was filled with the Holy Spirit and preached with the Holy Spirit's direction to people of Jerusalem, Samaria, and Judaea. His preaching was heard both by the Jews and the Samaritans. James, Peter, and John were present when Jesus raised Jairus's daughter back from death. They were the prominent and chosen Apostles and were present at the Agony of Gethsemani.

The Apostle James had a burning evangelical zeal for the gospel and preached to many in Israel and possibly Spain. His preaching was fearless, loud, forceful, effective, and he soon developed a reputation with the Jewish

Synagogues. He was challenging the Jewish leadership, their laws and beliefs and caused them to conspire with the Romans to have him silenced.

It was James' fiery preaching that helped to ignite the spread of the gospel throughout Israel and possibly in Spain. The Apostle James was a threat to the Jewish leadership and a problem for the Roman leadership. The Apostle James continually repeated that Jesus was the true Messiah and the Savior of the world. It was James and John who said yes to Jesus when he asked can you drink from the cup.

John 10:38 reads, "But Jesus said unto them, Ye know not what ye ask: can ye drink of the cup that I drink of? And be baptized with the baptism that I am baptized with?"

The Apostle James knew what drinking the cup meant and He wanted to give his life for the sake of the gospel. He lived his life for one purpose and that one purpose was to preach the saving grace of the Lord Jesus Christ. As the Apostle James walked to his death, he was preaching the gospel of Christ and spoke of his joy to serve His Savior and Lord, the Messiah.

It had been about 10 years since the Crucifixion of Jesus, and the death of the Apostle James would have had a traumatic impact on the Apostles. The death would have brought back the severe anguish and confusion when Jesus hung on the cross. They were reminded that their lives were in danger and especially now that King Herod realized that James' death curried favor from the Jews.

As Moses and Elijah, the Apostle James was a man of great courage. With God's blessing and the indwelling of the Holy Spirit, the Apostle James spoke fearlessly with great zeal that resulted in the conversion of many Jews. His message was clear then and today, God is calling all men to change their lives, to believe in Jesus, to run from evil, to ask for forgiveness, and to love your neighbor.

Today we need to renounce ourselves and eliminate any selfish pursuit that is preventing a closer relationship with our Lord and Creator. We are followers of Jesus and are following His example that was devoted to helping others that are in need and to share the gospel of grace to those that have ears to hear. There are people waiting to hear you speak and to share your testimony so they too may rejoice as the Apostle James. As the Apostle James, we need to be willing to drink the cup, which means to share His suffering and death and love, and to give ourselves in the service of others. We are able to drink the cup because Jesus went before us and showed us the way that we too will experience the joy, the blessings, and life everlasting.

The Apostle James as the older brother of the Apostle John was a man of God and the first Apostle to be martyred. Jesus loved the Apostle James for his zeal, his fearlessness, his courage, and his impact on the conversion of the Jews and the Gentiles.

PETER AS JESUS' WITNESS

The Apostle Peter was part of the inner circle and leader of the Apostles. Peter was the Apostle that first realized who Jesus was and was anxious to make that confirmation with Jesus and the other disciples.

Matthew 16:16 reads, "And Simon Peter answered and said, Thou art the Christ, The son of the living God."

Jesus acknowledged Peter as a person that would have a major impact on building the church and would be empowered by the Holy Spirit to heal and convert both Jews and Gentiles. The church would grow in numbers as the Apostle Peter and the other Apostles continued to preach the news that Jesus was the Messiah and that their salvation is free if only they believe.

Matthew 16:18 reads, "And I say also unto thee, That thou art Peter, and upon this rock I will build my church; and the gates of hell shall not prevail against it. And I will give thee the keys of the kingdom of heaven: and whatsoever thou shalt bind on earth shall be bound in heaven: and whatsoever thou shall loose on earth shall be loosed in heaven."

Jesus gave the Apostle Peter the keys to heaven. It was at the Day of Pentecost when the Apostle Peter first opened the door to heaven when he began to preach. The Apostle Peter was filled with the Holy Spirit and with God's authority when he began to share God's will for man and how salvation was available for all. Many that heard the Apostle's Peter's words that day believed and allowed the Holy Spirit to enter into their lives. The Apostle Peter had the privilege to announce to those who believed in the Lord Jesus Christ that their sins were forgiven and that the doors to heaven were open for them.

Matthew 16:21–22 reads, "From that time forth began Jesus to show unto his disciples, how that he must go unto Jerusalem, and suffer many things of the elders and chief priests and scribes, and be killed, and be raised again the third day. Then Peter took him, and began to rebuke him, saying, Be it far from thee, Lord: this shall not be unto thee."

Jesus had given the Apostles by this time the faith to withstand the pain and suffering that they would endure as their Savior and Lord was

The Transfiguration of Jesus

crucified. However, the Apostle Peter was distressed to hear this and did not understand why Jesus' death needed to take place.

Jesus had transformed Peter from a poorly educated man with few skills as a preacher to a man with great courage and faithfulness. He became part of the inner circle of Jesus' Apostles and was present during the Transfiguration. He achieved greatness within the church and held a special position. He began as a man with very humble beginnings and was able to achieve a special position within the church because of his solid rock faith in the Lord Jesus the Christ.

Peter was headstrong and would tell people what to do. He even attempted to tell Jesus what to do. He made many mistakes and was often impetuous and would talk before thinking. He denied Christ three times, he cut off the ear of the high priest's guard, and fell asleep in the garden as Jesus prayed.

However, Peter was also blessed by Jesus and was given the authority to heal and complete miracles. He was able to cast out demons and people were healed simply by believing and being in his presence.

Acts 9:40-43 reads, "But Peter put them all forth, and kneeled down, and prayed: and turning him to the body said, Tabitha, arise. And she opened her eyes, and when she saw Peter, she sat up. And he gave her his hand, and lifted her up, and when had called the saints and widows, presented her alive. And it was known throughout all Joppa; and many believed in the Lord. And it came to pass, that he tarred many days in Joppa with Simon a tanner."

Some of the personality traits that caused Peter many problems also worked to establish a base for greatness as a man of God.

Peter's denial of Christ haunted him and caused him to fall into complete repentance when Jesus asked him three times if he loved him. This reaffirmation allowed Peter to move from a fearful man to man of great maturity and courage. In a state of complete commitment he was able to grow in faith and benefit from a closer walk with his Lord and Savior. Peter's faith in Jesus was responsible for making a dramatic change in Peter from a fisherman to a great leader of the Christian church.

The Apostle Peter and the other Apostles were under pressure by the Roman and Jewish leadership for establishing a church that would challenge their own interests for both financial control and the leadership of the people. The Apostle Peter was eventually jailed and sentenced to death. He asked to be crucified upside down because he felt he was not worthy to be crucified in the same manner as his Lord.

We need to learn from The Apostle Peter and ask ourselves are we living a completely committed life that glorifies our Lord and Savior. As The Apostle Peter, we need to learn from our mistakes, grow in maturity, and become more courageous in our walk and in our ministry. We all make mistakes and we need to spend time in prayer to ask for forgiveness. God will transform us through the study of his word, allowing the Holy Spirit to speak to us, and to take time to recognize how the Holy Spirit works both in our lives and in the lives of others.

It was the Apostle Peter who recognized Jesus first at Galilee and could not wait for the boat and jumped into the sea to meet Jesus. It was the Apostle Peter who was the first to acknowledge Jesus as the Messiah. It was the Apostle Peter who quickly drew his sword to defend Jesus in the Garden of Gethsemane. And, it was God who sent an Angel to release the Apostle Peter from prison.

Acts 12:11 reads, "And when Peter was come to himself, he said, Now I know of a surely, that the hath sent his angel, and hath delivered me out of the hand of Herod, and from all the expectation of the people of the Jews."

JOHN AS JESUS' WITNESS

John was called the beloved Apostle by Jesus. He was the youngest of the Apostles and lived a long life, and is believed to have died in Ephesus at the age of 94. It is generally agreed that the Apostle John was responsible for writing the Gospel of John, three Epistles of John, and Book of Revelations. It is believed he moved from Israel between 33AD to 70AD with his family and extended family (include Mary the mother of Jesus) to support the Apostle Paul and the churches he started in Ephesus. The Apostle Paul died about 67 AD and the Apostle Peter died about 64 AD which left the Apostle John as the oldest original Apostle living from about 64 AD to 100 AD. This placed the Apostle John in the leadership role of the Ephesus church and subject to all the responsibilities. In about 95 AD he was banished to the Island of Patmos for a period of time and evidentially returned to the church of Ephesus.

John and his older brother the Apostle James (James the Greater) were also called by Jesus as the Sons of Thunder. Both men had little patience and when pushed to their limits would speak out loudly and chastise

The Transfiguration of Jesus

people for their sinful nature. However, both men were reprimanded by Jesus and they both seemed to be able to keep their temper under control. The Apostle Johns' writings do at times reflect shortness with those that do not believe and are not willing to change their lives. John's writings reflected a long life that was filled with many experiences such as the crucifixion of his Lord and Savior and other beloved Apostles, the death of his brother James, and the teachings of Jesus. The Apostle John's life was transformed, changing a young man with great intensity to an old man with great wisdom where faith became vision. These changes were made in spite of John's make-up. In other words Jesus is able mold a man into what he chooses regardless of past experiences.

The Apostle John was a student that sat at the feet of his Master for three years absorbing as much as humanly possible. He watched and experienced the washing of his feet by his Lord and Savior, Jesus. This simple act had a profound impact on John's understanding of what it meant to be a servant of the Lord. The fact that Jesus (God's only Son) would wash his feet, a task for a lowly servant, was difficult to understand, extremely humbling, and unbelievable. John was learning that we are servants to the gospel and that it is our mission in this life is to teach and preach the saving grace of God's word throughout the world. John grew to be a man of great passion, humility, and at the same time a man of great courage.

The Apostle John's life on the Island of Patmos was similar to that of Elijah. He lived in a cave where he was cut off from the outside world and was able to commune with his Lord and Savior. Both John and Elijah received prophetic revelations from God in this state where both men were being persecuted for preaching God's word. It was John being brandished to the Island of Patmos that allowed John to write the Book of Revelation.

Revelation 1:9 reads, "I John, who also am your brother, and companion in tribulation, and in the kingdom and patience of Jesus Christ, was in the isle that is called Patmos, for the word of god, and for the testimony of Jesus Christ."

The instruction John received from Jesus allowed him to serve his time on Patmos with an attitude of servitude, patience, and endurance knowing that his earthly experience would be met with grace and the glory of his heavenly Father.

The Apostle John was called the Beloved Apostle by Jesus. The Apostle John was passionate about the true word of God and how it affected all of God's creation. He was concerned about man's relationship with his

Heavenly Father and the need to love your neighbor, to be obedient God's word, and to be forgiving.

1 John 1:1–3 reads, "That which was from the beginning, which we have heard, which we have seen with our eyes, which we have looked upon, and our hands have handled, of the Word of Life. For the life was manifested, and we have we have seen it, and bear witness, and show unto you that eternal life, which was with the Father, and was manifested unto us. That which we have seen and heard declare we unto you, that ye also may have fellowship with us: and truly our fellowship is with the Father, and with his Son Jesus Christ."

The Apostle John was taught by Jesus, traveled and ate with Jesus, and was present when Jesus healed the sick, raised the dead, and cast out demons. He was witness to thousands being converted from a life of sin and death to a life full of eternal grace. These experiences changed the Apostle John in many ways. He became a person with a positive attitude, his focus was on others, and he was passionate about sharing God's truth with all of mankind regardless of the risks.

Ephesians 4:15 reads, "But speaking the truth in love, may grow up into him in all things, which is the head even Christ."

The Apostle John grew to be a man that spoke the word of God in love. God's words are spoken with the purpose of turning a life away from sin to a life of Grace. God's words are spoken in confidence, with grace, humility, and compassion. There is no room for pride, boasting, or self. When we see and hear the braggart, the boaster, the know it all, it is difficult to see anything beyond that lack of respect. We are to encourage one another to develop their gifts so that the church may grow and all may share in those gifts. The church is a living functioning body that is dependent on each member to engage and contribute their gifts.

The Apostle John was also aware of rejection by family and friends. The Apostles traveled with Jesus to Nazareth where he spent his childhood and spoke in the synagogue. Jesus read from Isaiah and explained that he was the Messiah.

Isaiah 61:1 reads, "The spirit of the Lord God is upon me; because the Lord hath anointed me to preach good tidings unto the meek; he hath sent me to bind up the broken hearted, to proclaim liberty to the captives, and the opening of the prison to them that are bound."

The family and friends of Jesus could only see that Jesus was the son of a carpenter and nothing more. They became offended by what Jesus

The Transfiguration of Jesus

was saying and forced him to leave the synagogue and Nazareth. Family dynamics are complex and involve a history of attitudes, opinions, and experiences. It is not uncommon for family members to resist or acknowledge success or changes made by another member. Some of these difficulties are psychosomatic and some are simply a refusal to acknowledge that sin exists and they need to consider allowing Jesus to resolve their many problems. The Apostle John was able to gain a deeper understanding from Jesus of the pain and anguish that one experiences when family and friends do not accept the gospel and the saving grace of the Lord Jesus.

The Apostle John was the head of the church of Ephesus for about 30 years. During this time The Roman Empire ruled the Mediterranean area with an iron fist. Any type of revolt or unrest was met with severe punishment by either death or imprisonment that resulted in thousands of Jews being slaughtered or being enslaved and sent to Rome. The Christians during this time were considered a cult that was responsible for unrest and conflicts with the Jews. Many of the people were highly superstitious and worshipped pagan gods and blamed the Christians for any hardship. In 64 AD the Christians were blamed for the great fire in Rome and as a result many were burned or put to death. In spite of all the persecution, the church grew during this 30 year period of time that Apostle John was head of the church. It has been estimated that 28% of the people in the area had heard God's word and it was preached in 6 different languages.

Ephesus was at that time the fourth greatest city in the region behind Rome, Alexandra, and Antioch. There was a massive temple built for the pagan goddess Diana (four times larger than the Parthenon) in Ephesus that drew thousands from around the region for all to worship for the promise of fertility, long life, and protection during child birth. Many celebrations were also held with music, dancing, singing and chanting. Many other temples and statues were also built for the pagan gods (i.e., Zeus, Apollo) for all to worship. The location of Ephesus and the temples created an economy based on worshiping of pagan gods. This economy involved trade, banking, collecting sacrificial funds for the gods, printing of money, prostitution, and other support businesses. The temple was administered by chief Priests and hundreds of other priests in support positions. It was to the financial benefit of the Roman Government to maintain and encourage the worship of the pagan gods.

The people that lived in and travel through Ephesus were polytheists and would worship many different pagan gods. They worshiped different pagan gods for different reasons (i.e., knowledge, wealth, and pleasure). The Apostle Paul, The Apostle John, The Apostle Timothy, and others had many challenges considering that the city of Ephesus had a society that was based on years of worship of pagan gods, a government that had financial interest in collecting funds at pagan temples, and that many people were very superstitious.

The Apostle John was living in a dangerous city where anyone could submit a compliant if they felt their livelihood was being threatened; someone was not showing respect to the mother goddess Diana, or claiming another god was more important than Ephesus' Goddess Diana. However, it is believed that the Jews were allowed citizenship and granted the freedom to practice their religious traditions. Paul and John did speak at the Jewish synagogue and at other locations around the Ephesus.

It was the Apostle John's ministry to encourage the Gentile Christians to realize the importance of their heavenly origin and their future with their Creator, but also to realize the responsibility to live a life on earth as those chosen of God and sealed by the Holy Spirit.

The Apostle John was a man of truth and taught the truth from the beginning for the purpose that all could have fellowship with The Holy Spirit, The Son and with The Father.

John 1:1–3 reads, "The beginning was the Word, and the Word was with God, and the Word was God. The same was in the beginning with God. All things were made by him; and without him was not any thing made that was made."

It was John's ministry that focused on the building up of the Gentiles and teaching them the law. The Apostle John's love for the church of Ephesus was repeated throughout his writings.

Revelations 2:1–6 reads, "Unto the angels of the church of Ephesus write; These things saith he that holdeth the seven stars in his right hand, who walketh in the midst of the seven golden candlesticks; I know thy works, and thy labor, and thy patience, and how thou canst not bear them which are evil: and thou hast tried them which say they are apostles, and are not, and hast found them liars. And hast borne, and hast patience, and for my names sake hast labored, and hast not fainted."

John's letter to the church was for the purpose of encouragement and love as they struggled to survive in a hostile environment where Christians were persecuted for any number of reasons. They were no longer strangers

The Transfiguration of Jesus

and foreigners, but they were now members of God's great kingdom of blessings that cannot be measured.

The Apostle John was persistently faithful throughout his entire life. It was Peter and John that ran together to the sepulcher the morning of the resurrection. The Apostle John experienced a great deal in his life. John changed because he had three years of training with his Savior and Lord; experienced the death and resurrection of his Savior and Lord, and saw Him later in His risen body. He experienced the death of his brother James and the death and beating of many more Apostles and early Christians. John's temperament grew to be one of great love and understanding. He was thoughtful and was able to sense God's will in each situation. John was a trusted Apostle that could be counted on and would be loved by all. It was John's love for the Church of Ephesus that caused his concern for all the members.

1 John 5:21 reads, "Little children keep yourselves from idols. Amen."

The pagan life in Ephesus was permeated with idols in virtually every aspect of daily life. It was only through the power of the Holy Spirit that these first converts to Christianity were able to separate themselves from pagan life and learn how to love others and obey God's commandments. It is only at that point when a true understanding of God's will is realized that a fervent love for others and a love for obedience exist.

The Apostle John and his life's work was centered on the truth and the fruit of the Holy Spirit and love.

John 3:16 reads, "For God so loved the world, that he gave his only begotten Son, that whosoever believeth in him should not perish, but have everlasting life."

John 14:15 reads, "If ye love me, keep my commandments."

1 John 3:10-11 reads, "In this the children of God are manifest, and the children of the devil: whosoever doeth not righteousness is not of God, nether he that loveth not his brother. For this is the message that ye heard from the beginning, that we should love one another."

1 John 4:7-12 reads, "Beloved, let us love one another: for love is of God; and everyone that loveth is born of God, and knoweth God. He that loveth not knoweth not God; for God is love. In this was manifested the love of God toward us, because that God sent his only begotten Son into the world, that we might live through him. Herein is love, not that we loved God, but that he loved us, and sent his Son to be the propitiation for our sin. Beloved, if God so loved us, we ought also to love one another. No man

hath seen God at any time. If we love one another, God dwelleth in us, and his love is perfected in us."

1 John 4:17-19 reads, "Herein is our love made perfect, that we may have boldness in the day of judgment: because as he is, so are we in this world. There is no fear in love; but perfect love casteth out fear: because fear hath torment. He that feareth is not made perfect in love. We love him, because he first loved us."

1 John 5:2-3 reads, "By this we know that we love the children of God, when we love God, and keep his commandments. For this is the love of God, that we keep his commandments: and his commandments are not grievous."

More than any other disciple the Apostle John spoke and wrote about loving your neighbor and following the commandments.

Matthew 22:37-40 reads, "Jesus said unto him, Thou shalt love Lord thy God with all thy heart, and with all thy soul, and with all thy mind. This is the first and greatest commandments. And the second is like unto it, thou shalt love thy neighbor as thyself. On these two commandments hang all the law and the prophets."

The Apostle John was following Jesus' teachings that loving the Lord God with all your heart, soul and mind is paramount for a person to begin a personal relationship with their Creator. This is a natural desire that God has placed within each person that cannot be filled by any accomplishment, possession, and any amount of wealth. The Holy Spirit will change each person that is willing to open their heart, soul, and mind and will convict them of the need to obey God's commandments.

The Apostle John spent his entire adult life teaching about God's love for His creation. The people of Ephesus were lost in a culture that worshiped stone idols in the hope that they would receive a better life. They had hundreds of priests that were well versed on mythology and would tell them about the many pagan gods and goddesses. However, there was no one that knew about Jesus Christ and the saving grace that was available to all of mankind. There was no one that knew that the Creator of all mankind sacrificed His Only Son so that all of mankind may be allowed access to life everlasting. There was no one that knew that the greatest commandment was to love God with all your heart, with your soul, and with all your mind. And, to love your neighbor as you would love yourself. Obviously, the Apostle John and the Church of Ephesus had the tremendous challenge

The Transfiguration of Jesus

to preach the message of the gospel under the continual threat of persecution and possible death.

The Ephesus church and the other churches in the area were struggling with people that knew only of the pagan gods that they had always worshiped. They were worshiping these pagan gods hoping their needs for food, shelter, pleasure, greed, wealth, and others would be met. There was pagan gods for every need including acts of perversion, satanic, and debauchery. There were few or no moral standards and the people were only subject to Roman Laws and the opinions of priests at the Ephesus' temples.

A pagan god is anything that prevents you from worshiping our Lord and Savior. Anything that takes priority or prevents you from worshiping our Lord and Savior is a pagan god. The people of today as the people of Ephesus are focused on self and experiencing as much pleasure as possible. The church is no longer a priority.

In Europe today you see many grand magnificent churches that are no longer used as churches. They are in many cases being maintained and managed by different governments. In some cases they are being destroyed or being used for other purposes rather than for worship. These churches were built by thousands of saints that sacrificed a great deal of time and money so that many generations may have a place to worship their Creator.

Unfortunately, today these churches are no longer attended due to a generation of people that are not interested in religion. The people of today have fallen prey to the same temptations that all men have fallen to since the beginning of time. They are focused on self and the worship of wealth, pleasure, status and anything that will satisfy their greed. These are the same issues that Moses, Elijah, Peter, James, and John had to deal with. Pagan gods have always been a temptation for man since they appeal to man's greed and sense of self.

The basic mission of the Apostle John as well as other saints was to minister to all of man that their Creator loved them and had provided a way for their salvation through his son Jesus the Christ. In addition, God was patiently waiting for them to realize that they needed to worship the all powerful, all knowing God, ever present God; their Creator.

The Apostle John was a loving and compassionate man that spent his life serving God's people and ministering the message of salvation to the world. It is believed that during his last years he was carried to church so that he may worship with the people of the church of Ephesus. It is believed that his last words were; children love one another.

9.

The Transfiguration

JESUS CHOSE PETER, JAMES, and John, the inner circle of Apostles, to travel with him for 6 to 8 days to a mountain (believed to be Mount Hermon) for the purpose of being witnesses to his Transfiguration. The Transfiguration is an event that compares with the Baptism, Crucifixion, Resurrection, and Ascension. During the Transfiguration both Moses and Elijah also appeared as witnesses to Jesus' Transfiguration.

Matthew 17:1–12 reads, "And after six days Jesus taketh Peter, James, and John his brother, and bringeth them up into a high mountain apart, And was transfigured before them: and his face did shine as the sun, and his raiment was white as the light. And, behold, there appeared unto them Moses and Elijah talking with him. Then answered Peter, and said unto Jesus, Lord, it is good for us to be here: if thou wilt, let us make here three tabernacles: one for thee, and one for Moses, and one for Elijah. While he yet spake, behold, a bright cloud overshadowed them and behold a voice out of the cloud, which said, This is my beloved Son, in whom I am well pleased: hear ye him. And when the disciples heard it, they fell on their face, and were sore afraid. And Jesus came and touched them, and said, "Arise, and be not afraid. And when they had lifted up their eyes, they saw no man, save Jesus only. And as they came down from the mountain, Jesus charged them, saying, Tell the vision to no man, until the Son of man be risen again from the dead. And his disciples asked him, saying, Why then say the scribes that Elijah must first come? And Jesus answered and said unto them, Elijah truly shall first come, and restore all things. But I say unto you, That Elijah is come already, and they knew him not, but have

The Transfiguration

done unto him whatsoever they listed. Likewise shall also the Son of man suffer of them."

The Apostles Peter, James, and John were witnesses to the Transfiguration of Jesus to his heavenly form. A form that was difficult to view because it was as bright as the sun and as white as pure light. As when Jesus was baptized; God speaks and said, "This is my beloved Son, in whom I am well pleased." The Apostles were petrified and were completely overcome by fear. However, being a witness to the Transfiguration gave new insights for the Apostles as to who Jesus was and how he was both a man and God's only Son.

The Transfiguration marks the beginning of the road of Jerusalem, the greatest miracle, the gift of eternal life for all of mankind through the Passion, the Crucifixion, the Resurrection, and the Ascension of Jesus the Christ. The Transfiguration allowed the Apostles to see Jesus as a deity and to realize he was able to defeat death and appear to them after the Resurrection.

The Transfiguration was also witnessed by Moses a man who was loved by God and was used by God to unfold his plan for the Jewish people. Moses was a great man of courage. Knowing that he could be put to death at any time he stood in front of the Pharaoh many times demanding the Jewish people's release from bondage.

Moses' presence at the Transfiguration also represented the Old Testament Law and how God's plan has been unfolding since the beginning of time. Moses was the tool that allowed God's love to release a complete generation of people from bondage and to allow the next generation to enter into the Promise Land.

The Old Testament introduces the gospel early in Genesis and outlines the fact that man will always be in a perpetual struggle with satanic forces. Man has the innate ability to know God's will, but will frequently disobey God's will due to the fact that man is easily confused by his basic need for greed, pleasure, and other self inspired desires.

Genesis 3:15 reads, "And I will put enmity between thee and the woman, and between thy seed and her seed; it shall bruise thy head, and thou shalt bruise his heel."

The fall of man has resulted in a struggle that will last throughout his entire life. Satan will strike the heel of man and cripple him. Man has many frailties and is completely dependent of God for direction in life and needs to obey God and his will.

God told Abraham that he would bless his people and protect them from evil.

Genesis 12:3 reads, "And I will bless them that bless thee, and curse him that curseth thee: and in thee shall all families of the earth be blessed."

Abraham obeyed God and began a journey with the Jewish people that would last for hundreds of years.

Genesis 22:11–18 reads, "And the angel of the Lord called unto him out of heaven, and said "Abraham, Abraham:" and he said, Here am I. And he said, Lay not thine hand upon the lad, neither do thou any thing unto him; for now I know that thou fearest God, seeing thou hast not withheld thy son, thine only son from me. And Abraham lifted up his eyes, and looked, and behold behind him a ram caught in a thicket by his horns: and Abraham went and took the ram, and offered him up for a burnt offering in the stead of his son. And Abraham called the name of that place Jebovah-jireh: as it is said to this day. In the mount of the Lord it shall be seen. And the angel of the Lord called unto Abraham out of heaven the second time, And said, By myself have I sworn, saith the Lord, for because thou hast done this thing, and hast not withheld thy son, thine only son; That in blessing I will bless thee, and in multiplying I will multiply thy seed as the stars of the heaven, and as the sand which is upon the seashore; and thy seed shall possess the gate of his enemies; And in thy seed shall all the nations of the earth be blessed; because thou hast obeyed my voice."

Abraham obeyed God and was willing to sacrifice his only son just as God was willing to sacrifice His only Son for us. Abraham's willingness to obey God has resulted in God's blessing for all of mankind throughout the entire world. The Old Testament acts as an introduction to the gospel of Christ and the saving grace that is available to all mankind.

Moses' appearance at the Transfiguration recognized that God's word was there from the beginning of time and that Jesus Christ Our Lord and Savior was the next step in the unfolding of God's will for all of His creation.

The other witness and representative of the Old Testament was Elijah. Just as Moses, Elijah was a great man of God. He was willing to face death as he confronted King Ahab and his wife Jezebel for commanding that all the people to worship the pagan god Baal and others.

The ministry of Elijah marks another major turning point in how God's plan for the Jewish people would be unfolding. The result of Elijah's courage and God's power to consume Elijah's altar was that thousands of Jews were able to once again worship their God, the true God. Elijah and

The Transfiguration

other prophets of the Old Testament were able to foretell the coming of the Messiah.

Micah 5:2 reads, "But thou, Bethlehem Ephratah, though thou be little among the thousands of Judah, yet out of thee shall he come forth unto me that is to be ruler in Israel; whose goings forth have been from of old, from everlasting."

The prophet foretold that the one born in Bethlehem would be the ruler for all of eternity.

Isaiah 7:14 reads, "Therefore the Lord himself shall give you a sign; Behold, a virgin shall conceive, and bear a son, and shall call his name Immanuel."

The prophet foretold God's only Son would be born of a virgin.

Isaiah 9:6–7 reads, "For unto us a child is born, unto us a son is given: and the government shall be upon has shoulder: and his name shall be called Wonderful, Counselor, The mighty God, The everlasting Father, The Prince of Peace. Of the increase of his government and peace there shall be no end, upon the throne of David, and upon his kingdom, to order it, and to establish it with judgment and with justice from henceforth even for ever. The zeal of the Lord of hosts will perform this."

God incarnate through His Son would be born as a child and would bring eternal life to those who will believe and obey His commandments.

Elijah represents the prophets and the prophecies that God will offer His Son as the ultimate sacrifice to pay for all of the sins of mankind. It is only that gift that allows man the opportunity to enter into the kingdom of God.

Isaiah 53:3–7 reads, "He is despised and rejected of men; a man of sorrows, and acquainted with grief: and we hid as it were our faces from him; he was despised, and we esteemed him not. Surely he hath borne our griefs, and carried our sorrows: yet we did esteem him stricken, smitten of God, and afflicted. But he was wounded for our transgressions, he was bruised for our iniquities: the chastisement of our peace was upon him; and with his stripes we are healed. All we like sheep have gone astray; we have turned every one to his own way; and the Lord hath laid on him the iniquity of us all. He was oppressed, and he was afflicted, yet he opened not his mouth: he is brought as a lamb to the slaughter, and as a sheep before her shearers is dumb, so he opened not his mouth."

The prophet explains in detail the suffering of mankind's Lord and Savior will endure for the payment for all of mankind's sins. Jesus the Christ was this lamb that was slaughtered and with his wounds we were healed.

Elijah the prophet was a witness to the Transfiguration for the purpose of representing the hundreds of prophecies that were made by many prophets to foretell the coming of God's only Son, Jesus the Christ. Elijah as Moses was a godly man that had great courage to demand that the Jewish people be allowed to worship their God, the true God. Elijah had a tremendous impact on moving the Jewish people from worshiping pagan gods back to worshiping their true God.

The three Apostles that were witnesses to the Transfiguration were Peter, James (the greater), and John. These three Apostles were considered the inner circle for the Apostles at this time. The Apostle Peter was a man of great commitment to Jesus and at the same time a man with many human frailties. The Apostle Peter was the leader for the Apostles and had great love for his Lord and Savior, but at times was confused and overcome by fear. He was a man of great passion, zeal, and at times even impetuous.

The Apostle Peter was a witness to the Transfiguration because he was the first to proclaim Jesus as the Messiah, he was the first to recognize Jesus on the shore and jump into the Sea of Galilee, he was the first to run and enter the empty tomb, and the first to draw his sword to defend Jesus in the garden. He grew to be a man with unquestionable dedication to his Master, and his unwavering faith through the Holy Spirit allowed him to complete miracles. His preaching at Pentecost resulted in thousands of souls receiving eternal life.

Acts 2:38–40 reads, "Then Peter said unto them, Repent, and be baptized every one of you in the name of Jesus Christ for the remission of sins, and ye shall receive the gift of the Holy Ghost. For the promise is unto you, and to your children, and to all that are afar off, even as many as the Lord our God shall call. And with many other words did he testify and exhort, saying, Save yourselves from this untoward generation."

The Apostle Peter with the baptism of the Holy Spirit convicted thousands to realize that Jesus was their Lord and Savior. They needed to repent of their sins, to admit they were sinners, to confess all that was sin, and to turn away from sin.

The Crucifixion of Jesus was heavy on the Apostle Peter's heart. The Apostle and many others realized how deceptive the Chief Priest was in distorting the issue to cause an innocent, peaceful, and righteous man

The Transfiguration

without any sin to be crucified. Peter and the other Apostles began to realize that Jesus' crucifixion showed the High Priest to be extremely corrupt and perverse. The Temple authorities were capable of doing anything to maintain their position and control over the Temple and Jewish people. The High Priest also maintained a relationship with the Roman Empire even though they were deeply involved in worshiping pagan gods.

The early Christian church was in some cases meeting in the temples and following many of the Jewish traditions. Peter, John, and James were also involved in the early church and were involved in preaching and teaching about Jesus Christ and the prophecies of the coming of the Messiah found in the Old Testament. However, over time this relationship changed as more of the Jewish leadership became aware of the number of people that were converting to Christianity. It is believed that hatred grew within the Jewish community for the Temple priest for their lack of not following Jewish law and the Torah. The Temple authorities reacted by starting a campaign to discredit the Jesus followers as heretics, and people wanting to destroy Judaism.

From that point further the situation deteriorated for the early church in Jerusalem and those that followed Jesus to the point when the Apostle James (the greater) was martyred in 44 AD by King Agrippa (Herod). The Romans realized this execution found favor with the Temple leadership and continued their persecution of the followers of Jesus. Herod then began to arrest those that belong to the Christian church including the Apostle Peter. It was Herod's intent to put the Apostle Peter on public trial to gain greater favor from the Temple authorities.

Acts 12:7–8 reads, "And behold, the angel of the Lord came upon him, and a light shined in the prison: and he smote Peter on the side, and raised him up, saying, Arise up quickly, And his chains fell off from his hands. And the angel said unto him, Gird thyself, and bind on thy sandals. And so he did. And he saith unto him, Cast thy garment about thee, and follow me."

God sent this angel to free Peter from this prison for the purpose of allowing Peter to continue his work of building the church.

Acts 12:12 reads, "And when he had considered the thing, he came to the house of Mary the mother of John, whose surname was Mark, where many were gathered to together praying."

Peter stood at the door knocking, but they did not believe it could be Peter. Eventually, they let him in and Peter explained how an angel came and freed him from the prison.

When Herod discovered that Peter had escaped from prison he had his guards put to death. From that point in time, God, His angels, the Apostles, and the early Christians all worked to protect the Apostle Peter from the death sentence that was on his head. The Apostle Peter quickly traveled away from Jerusalem and began building churches around the Mediterranean Sea area.

There is little or no biblical support to where the Apostle Peter traveled to after leaving the Apostle John and the group of believers. John and the family of believers would have naturally assisted Peter with all of his needs (e.g., money, clothing) and would have made plans for his escape from Jerusalem. There is no mention of the Apostle Peter at the church of Ephesus, Corinth, Galatia, or others after this time period (44AD). It is also at this point in time that we see dramatic differences in opinions as to where the Apostle Peter traveled.

At this point we see a greater dependence on church tradition and documentation that has been accumulated from many different sources. There was a larger Jewish community in Rome that could have provided support and assistance to Peter in establishing himself within the city of an estimated 1 million people.

During this time Mark the disciple and interpreter of the Apostle Peter wrote the Gospel of Mark. The First Epistle of 1 Peter and The Second Epistle of Peter are believed to have been written by the Apostle Peter to a number of churches that were being persecuted in Asia Minor. The Gospel of Mark was directed primarily at the Gentiles that were converted by the Apostle Peter. It is believed that the Apostle Paul worked with Peter in establishing Christian churches for both the Jews and the Gentiles. It is also believed and documented by church tradition that both Peter and Paul were imprisoned in the Roman prison Tullianum. The Apostle Peter requested that he be crucified upside down in 64 AD because he was not worthy to be crucified as his Savior and Lord.

The Apostle Peter (the prince of Apostles) was a man that Jesus loved and blessed with the power to change men from worshiping pagan gods to worshiping the one true God. The Apostle Peter lead the Apostles by allowing them to realize that they were being kept by the power of God through faith. He instructed them as to how to grow in faith and to realize it was

The Transfiguration

more valuable then gold. Faith is priceless and a gift from God that allows mankind to realize eternal life.

1 Peter 5:6–10 reads, "Humble yourselves therefore under the mighty hand of God, that he may exalt you in due time. Casting all your care upon him; for he careth for you. Be sober, be vigilant; because the devil, as a roaring lion, walketh about, seeking whom he may devour. Whom resist steadfast in the faith, knowing that the same of afflictions are accomplished to your brethren are accomplished in brethren that are in the world. But the God of all grace, who hath called us unto his eternal glory by Christ Jesus, after that ye have suffered a while, make you perfect, stablish, strengthen, settle you."

The Apostle Peter was instructing this early church to humble themselves and to admit that they need God's strength to carry them through the persecution they were experiencing. Peter reminds them that many are experiencing this persecution and they are not standing alone against Satan and demons. Peter also reminds them that in order to grow in strength you need to experience some challenges. The grace of God becomes one with man and perfects man as he struggles against the evil that exists in this world. The suffering that is experienced in this world only last for a short period of time and cannot be compared to eternal life that lasts forever.

The Apostle Peter represented common man at the Transfiguration. Peter was a common fisherman from Galilee with many of man's frailties that was transformed from Peter the fisherman to the Apostle Peter. Peter was transformed from an independent, self-willed, presumptuous, and braggart to a humble servant, directed by God's Holy Spirit. The Apostle Peter became a man motivated by the love for his fellowman through the grace that was provided through the resurrection of the living Savior and Lord.

Peter was not a Temple Priest, Rabbi, scholar, or even well versed in Jewish law. However, Jesus chose this fisherman from Galilee and transformed him into the leader of the Apostles. No one expected this man to become the greatest teacher of humility, submission, hope, and love for your fellowman. It is through God's grace and wisdom that a man like Peter can be spiritually converted from being a fisherman to being one of the greatest spiritual leaders in the history of man.

The Apostle James (son of Zebedee), older brother of John the Apostle was another witness to the Transfiguration. He was known as one of the "Sons of Thunder" because of his desire to call down fire to destroy a

Samarian village for not welcoming Jesus on his journey. The Apostle James was one of Jesus' favorites because of his enthusiasm and zeal for preaching the message of salvation through the Messiah Jesus Christ. The Apostle James at the Transfiguration represents the drinking of the chalice and the resulting persecution and execution of the Apostles.

Acts 12:1-2 reads, "Now about that time Herod the king stretched forth his hands to vex certain of the church. And he killed James the brother of John with the sword."

The Apostle James like John his brother was a man of great courage that delivered fiery messages that confronted Jewish beliefs and caused many to convert to Christianity. James along with Peter and John were considered to be in the inner circle of Apostles and received instruction directly from Jesus for three years. The Apostle James was at the miracle of Jairus' daughter, with Jesus during his agony in the Garden of Gethsemane, and was painfully aware of the Crucifixion and the glorification of the Resurrection.

The Apostle James was a fire that ignited the spread of the gospel throughout the Mediterranean area. He spoke without fear and delivered message after message that explained that Jesus was the Messiah and that anyone who wished to have eternal life needed to repent of their sins, and ask God to direct their daily life. He did not hesitate, he did slow down, he knew the risks, and he spoke directly and forcefully as a man with limited time. The Apostle James was glorified as the first Apostle to be martyred.

As with Moses, Elijah, and Peter, the Apostle James was a man of great courage that was completely and utterly dependent on God for his strength and direction.

We are all on the same path, as the Apostle James spoke of the Savior and Lord, so do we put our faith as we walk the pilgrimage of the Christian life. The Apostle James realized that Jesus had given him this opportunity to be a messenger of God's word. He needed to be as effective as possible to insure that everyone that heard him would know that Jesus was the Messiah and that he defeated death by his death and Resurrection so that all men may experience eternal life. The Apostle James was martyred in 44AD only 14 years after he accepted the challenge of drinking from the chalice that Jesus drank from.

Matthew 16:21-26 reads, "From that time forth began Jesus to show unto his disciples, how that he must go unto Jerusalem, and suffer many things of the elders and chief priests and scribes, and be killed, and be raised again the third day. Then Peter took him, and began to rebuke him, saying, Be it far from thee, Lord, this shall not be unto thee. But he turned, and said unto Peter, Get thee behind me, Satan: thou art an offense unto me: for thou savorest not the things that be of God, but those that be of men. Then Jesus unto his disciples, If any man will come after me, let him deny himself, and take up his cross, and follow me. For whosoever will save his life shall lose it, and whosoever will lose his life for my sake shall find it. For what is a man profited, if he shall gain the whole world, and lose his own soul? Or what shall a man give in exchange for his soul?"

The Apostle James understood Jesus' teachings and realized that his sole purpose in this life was to tell others about what God had done for all of mankind, regardless of his preoccupation with self and his desires. It was the relationship he had with his Savior and Lord that was important and not his position in this life and his possessions. The Apostle James faith was unwavering and he was completely committed to reaching as many people as possible.

The Apostle John (the Apostle James young brother) had experienced great sorrow with the Crucifixion of his Lord and Savior and great joy with the Resurrection of his Savior, the conversions of thousands of souls, and the growth of the church. The Apostle John certainly experienced a great deal more than any other Apostle partly due to reaching the age of about 94. He was the head of the church for many years after the death of both the Apostle Peter and the Apostle Paul and many others. The Apostle John spoke directly to the souls of many generations about God's truth and that true joy was only realized with a close relationship with your Lord and Savior,

John 15:11 reads, "These things have I spoken unto you, that my joy might remain in you, and that your joy might be full."

The Apostle John (John the evangelist, John the beloved) had a heart of love that was continually focused on God's truth. John's desire for all mankind was that they might experience true joy, that their joy may be overflowing and holy, and that they may experience a faith that is unshakable.

John 3:15 reads, "That whosoever believeth in him should not perish, but have eternal life."

The Apostle John speaks in clear terms and explains that we are confronted with either good or evil, light or dark, life or death, receiving or rejecting Christ, and salvation or damnation. The decision is great and consequences are enormous. At the end those that had repented of their sin will leave their bodies and be met by an endless radiant light. They will not be ashamed as the light reveals all that they have done throughout their life.

John was a man of great courage and commitment which was apparent at the cross. It was The Apostle John and Mary (mother of Jesus) that stood at the foot of the cross while other apostles were in hiding. John loved the church and always encouraged its members to spend time in prayer and study. He was very loving and patient with people and at the same time straight forward in dealing with sin and any attempt to distort God's word. The Apostle lived during a very dangerous and challenging time with people worshiping pagan gods and practicing satanic rituals. John had a servant's attitude and at the same time spent a great deal of time in prayer. His knowledge of scripture was more than just academic it was spiritually inspired.

The Apostle John had a major influence on the early church and its growth throughout the Mediterranean area and Europe to the current church throughout the world. It was The Apostle John and others that recognized the Apostle Paul and Barnabas for their great success in building the early church.

Galatians 2:9 reads, "And when James, Cephas, and John, who seemed to be pillars, perceived the grace that was given unto me, they gave to me and Barnabas the right hands of fellowship; that we should go unto the heathen, and they unto the circumcision."

The Apostle John recognized the Apostle Paul's great work and ensured that the grace of God would be a benefit to all of the early Gentile believers including the desperately poor Jewish believers in Jerusalem. The Apostle John was a spiritual leader that ensured all believers were recognized equally and treated with love, respect, and consideration.

The Apostle John understood that the word of God became man in the form of His only Son Jesus Christ.

John 1:14 reads, "And the word was made flesh, and dwelt among us, and we beheld his glory, the glory as of the only begotten of the Father, full of grace and truth."

John had been with those that had seen the glory of the Transfiguration and had seen the glory of the Son of God. He had experience the divine true word of God and realized God's word was wrapped in the love for all of mankind.

THE TRANSFIGURATION

SUMMARY

The witnesses to the Transfiguration were men inspired by God and His Son the Lord Jesus Christ. Moses, Elijah, Peter, James, and John were men of great courage that we cannot imagine. Each one of these men confronted great leaders that possessed the power to execute these men of God at any time. Their contributions to the gospel were enormous as they fought against Satan, his demons and principalities. The one common enemy they all fought against was the worship of pagan gods that we are still battling today. Men are still worshiping wealth, possessions, pleasures, and many more pagan gods. The worship of the pagan gods separates man from God and prevents the worship of the one and only true God. This separation will continue to have enormous consequences for these individuals as it will result in an eternal separation.

God took each of these men and transformed them from men with few skills to men that were great leaders, writers, speakers, and evangelists. No one would select these individuals based on their prior occupations or education. God looked at individuals as to what they would become. Moses was a shepherd in the wilderness when God confronted him in a burning bush. Elijah was a priest that lived off the land and took shelter in caves. Peter, James, and John were common fisherman with little formal education. God with His Son Jesus Christ and the Holy Spirit will in some cases make dramatic changes in a person life if they are willing to accept His direction.

These men were men that had proven themselves to be completely committed to God and His Son Jesus Christ. They were selected by God to be witnesses to the Transfiguration because they were representatives of God's plan for man and because of their love for their Creator. Peter, James, and John were present to see Jesus in all his glory and to realize Jesus was God's only Son their Lord and Master. The Transfiguration of Jesus would be seared into the Apostles memory and marked the beginning of the journey by Jesus the Christ to Jerusalem. There in Jerusalem God's greatest gift to all of mankind would be realized with the sacrifice of His beloved Son, Jesus the Christ.

God accepts all of man's frailties and will direct and comfort them in every aspect of their life. Moses in some respects was a broken man with little or no confidence and a temper he could not control. He ran for his life after killing an Egyptian guard and lived for forty years in fear in the wilderness. He could not speak clearly and had problems explaining his thoughts. However, God wanted Moses included in his plan regardless of his many human frailties; provided Moses with Aaron for support, and God instilled in Moses great courage that only God could provide. The transformation of Moses was a miracle and shows that all things are possible for those who are willing to place their faith in the one true God. Moses was a man who was leading sheep when God confronted and directed him to return to Egypt and to lead over 600,000 Jews out of slavery under the Pharaoh's rule. The idea of demanding the Pharaoh to release his slaves is incomprehensible and does not seem possible. However, nothing is impossible with God. God is able to take any man regardless of his background and status in society and transform him into accomplishing great things within God's plan.

Mark 10:27 reads, "And Jesus looking upon them saith, With men it is impossible, but not with God: for with God all things are possible."

We need to keep our eyes on God and not on man and the things of this earth. God is patiently waiting for us to say, Here I am God take me.

Moses was selected to be a witness to Jesus' Transfiguration due to the fact he surrendered all to God and followed His direction. He became an obedient servant and in doing so lead the Israelites out of Egypt and delivered the law (Ten Commandments) to a people that was completely lost in worshiping pagan gods.

Elijah, a priest and prophet was a man with little or no income and lived off the land and found shelter in caves. God selected Elijah to confront King Ahab and his wife Jezebel because of their ruling to force all to worship the pagan god Baal and others. Elijah although desperately poor with no possessions, was loved by God and honored with a great task.

Again, we see God use a man that is not successful nor holds a prominent position in public office. Elijah was a man that had a close relationship with God and in many respects completely dependent on God for his survival. As Moses, Elijah was a man of great commitment to God and of great courage. He obeyed God and confronted King Ahab and demanded that the Jewish people be allowed to worship their own God. Elijah also prophesied that God would bring a three year drought that would result in destruction of all of the crops and create a great famine for years. This type of prophecy by Elijah was met with great anger by the King and put his life in immediate danger.

God used Elijah to build a sacrificial altar to God for the purpose of revealing God's power and glory to His people. Elijah prayed throughout the day and at the end of the day God poured down fire that consumed the entire altar. This miracle caused thousands of God's people to convert to worshiping the true God and revolt against the King's ruling. This conversion of thousands represented a new beginning for many of God's people and a new future for those in Israel. It was that conversion of God's people and God's miracle for a new beginning that was represented by Elijah at the Transfiguration of Jesus.

Both Moses and Elijah were confronted by God's people worshiping pagan gods. The fallen man is weak and has many frailties. He is easily distracted by any number of temptations, the most prevalent being money, possessions, status, and pleasure.

Matthew 6:33 reads, "But seek ye first the kingdom of God, and his righteousness; and all these things shall be added unto you."

The message is clear that man's first priority is to seek God's righteousness, grace and mercy and He will then provide for your needs.

Matthew 6:34 reads, "Take therefore no thoughts for the morrow: for the morrow shall take thought for the things of itself. Sufficient unto the day is the evil thereof."

Again, the message is clear that we should not be spending time worrying about tomorrow and the hypothetical. We need to be concerned about today and the issues that need our full attention and prayers. The pagan has no faith in God and His promises and will spend his entire life worried and seeking pleasure and peace.

The three Apostles Peter, James, and John were all selected by Jesus to be witnesses to the Transfiguration. The Apostle Peter was a common man with all the frailties of a common man. He failed many times, but yet God was patient and blessed him as the leader of the Apostles. The Apostle Peter grew from being a man that was quick to act without first understanding the issue to being a man with great God given wisdom that had a profound effect on leading the other Apostles and on growing the early church. The Apostle James was a common fisherman that God changed into a great speaker that delivered fiery message after fiery message that caused great consternation within the Jewish community. He was hated by the Temple authorities and the high priest. James was a man with great courage and faith that strengthened him to deliver the message of salvation to all he encountered.

Ephesians 3:20–21 reads, "Now unto him that is able to do exceeding abundantly above all that we ask or think, according to the power that worketh in us. Unto him be glory in the church by Christ Jesus throughout all ages, world without end. Amen."

The Holy Spirit was manifested within the Apostle James and allowed him to deliver messages that changed the life of many. We need to allow the Holy Spirit to speak through us and not to limit or prevent His plan or purpose. The Apostle James was a vessel that the Holy Spirit indwelled and filled for His purpose.

The Apostle John was another common man with all the faults of a common man, but God selected him and changed him to speak and write about God's greatest gift for all of mankind.

10.

Application

THE WITNESSES FOR THE Transfiguration were all common men with all the faults of an average person. However, God selected these men to be witnesses to one of the greatest miracles because of what they had accomplished and what they would accomplish through Him. God selected these men because they were common men without any social status and had hearts that were open to God's direction. The prerequisite for being used by God is being void of pride and a love for the things of this world. The message from God, His word, and the sacrifice of His Son is a message that is completely contrary to the world's values. God's first priority for us is to praise Him, to have a thankful heart, and to worship Him. Anything that that prevents this is considered sin.

1 John 2:15–17 reads, "Love not the world, neither the things that are in the world. If any man love the world, the love of the Father is not in him. For all that is in the world, the lust of the flesh, and the lust of the eyes, and the pride of life, is not of the Father, but is of the world. And the world passeth away, and the lust thereof: but he that doeth the will of God abideth for ever."

We need to be vigilant and not let the world distract us from keeping our first priority of worshiping God. There are millions of pagans today that spend their entire lives worshiping everything other than God. Anything that prevents a person from worshiping God is a pagan god. Unfortunately, there are many that call themselves Christians.

Many of today's churches only present a partial view of God's character and His will for His people. Many churches of today do not mention sin and God's view of sin fearing they will offend or alienate some members.

Consequently, many attending churches today are left thinking they can continue their sinful ways without fear of God's wrath.

Proverbs 6:16–19 reads, "These are things doth the Lord hate; yes, seven are an abomination unto him. A proud look, a lying tongue, and hands that shed innocent blood, A heart that deviseth wicked imaginations, feet that be swift in running to mischief, A false witness that speaketh lies, and he that soweth discord among brethren."

Proverbs 8:13 reads, "The fear of the Lord is to hate evil: pride, and arrogancy, and the evil way, and the forward mouth, do I hate."

We all have seen the pompous and self serving as they try to fulfill their desire for recognition.

The pride of life is contrary to almost everything the Bible teaches and what the church should be instructing its' members. Today the world and Satan are continually working hard to convince people to honor those that take advantage of others, those that scheme and cheat, and those that kill the innocent. And, there are those that try to find self worth and recognition by discrediting others with the collection and dissemination of personal information.

Colossians 3:23–24 reads, "And whatsoever ye do, do it heartily, as to the Lord, and not unto men. Knowing that of the Lord ye shall receive the reward of the inheritance: for ye serve the Lord Christ."

We are God's creation and we do all things to honor Him and praise His name. Our hearts are focused on pleasing God and not man or our selves. We were created with talents and we need to use them wisely for the purpose of honoring our Lord and Savior. We are part of God's family effectively using our God given talents to help and provide for our neighbor. Our priority is to love God and our neighbor.

God said, "anyone that hates his brother is a murderer."

1 John 3:15 reads, "Whosoever hateth his brother is murderer: and ye know that no murderer hath eternal life abiding in him."

God and His Holy Spirit will not dwell in us as Christians if we hate our neighbor. We become as an empty shell without His Spirit to love us and comfort us. If we hate our neighbor we lose our communion with our Lord and we revert back to the world and the desires of the world.

However, God has provided us with instructions as to how to live a righteous life. It is God's endless mercies that allows us to fail again and again and still remain sealed in His grace.

APPLICATION

Romans 12:1-2 reads, "I beseech you therefore brethren, by the mercies of God, that ye present your bodies a living sacrifice, holy, acceptable unto God, which is your reasonable service. And be not conformed to this world: but be ye transformed by the by the renewing of your mind, that ye may prove what is that good, and acceptable, and perfect, will of God."

At the moment you admit you are a sinner and ask Jesus Christ to enter into your life you become a changed person. The Holy Spirit will cause you to change your thoughts and attitudes and see things from a different perspective. Your language will change along with what you consider appropriate to discuss. Your heart will change and you will show greater love and compassion for your neighbors. You will be increasingly sensitive to and repulsed by gossip and slander.

God saw in these men (Moses, Elijah, Peter, James, and John) not only their potential, but their basic character traits that would make them acceptable as wittinesses to one of the greatest miracles. Those basis character traits would include, love, joy, peace, forbearance, kindness, goodness, fruitfulness, gentleness, and self-control.

LOVE FOR YOUR NEIGHBOR

Certainly all of these men were men that exhibited great love for their neighbors as they lived their lives in submission to God's direction. Moses' love and compassion for the Israelites and their bondage made him a man that God could use and build into a great leader for the Israelites. It was The Apostle James' desire and love for God's people that allowed him to deliver such fiery sermons that those that were in ear shot were moved and recognized that he was speaking of God's truth. The Apostle Peter's love for Jesus was unquestionable. Among the Apostles, Peter was the first in many ways to express his love for Jesus. He was the first to recognize Jesus as the Messiah and the Savior for all mankind. Peter was impetuous and his love for Jesus was obvious as he jumped into the water because he could not wait for the boat to arrive. The Apostle Peter made many mistakes, but Jesus loved him regardless. When Jesus asked Peter three times if he loved him he was devastated. And, when a broken Peter said yes, Jesus said, feed my sheep. The Apostle Peter spent the next 40 years feeding Jesus' sheep showing his love for both His Lord and neighbor. The Apostle John was a man that Jesus loved for his ability to grasp the importance of biblical truths and teachings. John was a compassionate man and had a heart for those in need.

John 13:1 reads, "Now before the feast of the Passover, when Jesus knew that his hour was come that he should depart out of this world unto the Father, having loved his own which were in the world, he loved them unto the end."

No greater love has ever been seen as when God gave His only Son. No greater humility as ever been experienced as when God's only Son became a servant and teacher to His people. And, finally Jesus' obedience, death, and Resurrection revealed a love that defeated death and will never end.

The example of love has been presented for us to follow. All of these selected witnesses (Moses, Elijah, Peter, James, and John) were all obedient servants. They all understood the importance of listening and understanding God's word and direction. Moses and Elijah were completely dependent on God for their daily existence. Peter, James, and John were also dependent on God as they preached God's word in a hostile environment where death was a possibility any day. All these men loved their neighbors and were willing to make the ultimate sacrifice so that they may experience eternal life with their Creator.

We need to remember that the greatest gift is God's love for us and we need to share that gift with our neighbors. There is nothing we could do that would have a greater impact on their lives than to explain the way of salvation. The consequence of this decision is life or death and will last for eternity. Unfortunately, many churches are adrift today and spend more time speaking of social issues and in some cases nothing about salvation. We all need to be prepared to answer the question, have you fed my sheep? What kind of shepherd have you been for God's people? Have you been loving, caring, and thoughtful of others? Have you been willing to be protective of others from the wolves of this world, are you willing to give a helping hand to others, and are you willing to go after the one that is lost?

JOY OF THE SPIRIT

The spiritual joy we experience in our daily lives is controlled by the Holy Spirit within our being. The Holy Spirit communes with us in a way we cannot understand and intercedes for us in our prayers. Unfortunately, the degree and consistency of spiritual joy within our life is affected by sin. Sin has an immediate effect on the Holy Spirit and will quench the spirit and diminish our spiritual joy.

Application

The degree of spiritual joy will fluctuate and will react to highly spiritual music, preaching, or other messages of God's love and compassion. It is not uncommon for people to be overcome by Spiritual Joy.

Deuteronomy 4:37-39 reads, "And because he loved thy fathers, therefore he chose their seed after them, and brought thee out in his sight with his mighty power out of Egypt. To drive out nations from before thee greater and mightier that thou art, to bring thee in, to give thee their land for an inheritance, as it is this day. Know therefore this day, and consider it in thine heart, that the Lord he is God in heaven above, and upon the earth beneath: there is none else."

As Moses, we need to consider all of God's blessings and realize that He is the one and only God and the Creator of all. Moses had great spiritual joy when he saw what God had done for the Israelites.

Exodus 15:1-5 reads, "Then sang Moses and the children of Israel this song unto the Lord, and spake, saying, I will sing unto the Lord, saying, for he hath triumphed gloriously: the horse and his rider hath he thrown into the sea. The Lord is my strength and song, and he becomes my salvation: he is my God, and I will prepare him a habitation; my father's God, and I will exalt him. The Lord is man of war: the Lord is his name. Pharaoh's chariots and his host hath he cast into the sea: his chosen captains also are drowned in the Red Sea. The depths have covered them: they sank into the bottom as a stone."

Moses and the Israelites sang a song of great joy and praise knowing that the hand of the Lord had protected them from Pharaoh's army and certain death and slavery. We know that the Creator of the universe with His mighty powers and with greatness of majesty is our personal Lord and Savior and that He has placed His hand of protection over us each day. He has personally directed us away from the Pharaoh's of this world. Our hearts are full of spiritual joy as we sing and praise our Lord and Savior. We fall on our faces as we ask for redemption from our pride of life and our sin nature.

Elijah was a man who wrestled with his expectations for how events should unfold. It wasn't until he realized that God was in control regardless of his own expectations that he was able to fully understand and appreciate the sweet comfort of spiritual joy. God is in control as to how events unfold. We are responsible for being obedient to God's word, to submit our requests in prayer, and to be faithful in all things. We rest in Him putting all of our trust in Him knowing He loves us and is preparing our way.

2 Corinthians 5:5–7 reads, "Now he that hath wrought us for the selfsame thing is God, who also hath given unto us the earnest of the spirit. Therefore we are always confident, knowing that, whilst we are at home in the body, we are absent for the Lord. For we walk by faith, not by sight."

Our spirits long to be with our Creator and Lord. And, we experience spiritual joy when we hear His words in song, in testimony, and in reading. Our spiritual joy increases as we learn to view our life in its proper perspective. We need to focus on the final goal and prepare ourselves for an eternal life with our Lord and Savior.

Peter realized that spiritual joy can be realized when fear has been conquered through faith.

1 Peter 1:6 reads, "Wherein ye greatly rejoice, though now for a season, if need be, ye are in heaviness through manifold temptations."

When we succeed against temptations we grow in faith and we experience spiritual joy. Faith grows stronger when tested with trials and temptations and we finally realize we can always put our faith in the Lord to carry us through any situation.

God changed Peter from a selfish, self-centered man with many frailties into a spirit-filled vessel capable of healing those with infirmities. Peter's spiritual joy was experienced with trials and struggles knowing God was pruning away his sinful nature.

1 Peter 4:13 reads, "But rejoice, inasmuch as ye are partakers of Christ's sufferings; that, when his glory shall be revealed, ye may be glad also with exceeding joy."

1 Peter 1:7 reads, "That the trial of your faith, being much more precious than of gold that perisheth, though it be tried with fire, might be found unto praise and honor and glory at the appearing of Jesus Christ."

We run a race with thousands of spectators in heaven cheering us on as we strengthen our endurance with each new problem and issue that hinders our progress. We are waiting to hear the words, "well done my good and faithful servant."

Matthew 25:21 reads, "His Lord said unto him, Well done, thou good and faithful servant: thou hast been faithful over a few things, I will make thee ruler over many things: enter thou into the joy of thy Lord."

The Apostle James' (Son of Thunder) spiritual joy was amazing. He was the oldest Apostle and one of the most spiritually mature with a gift for speaking. His heart was fixed on delivering the message of salvation to all who would listen and his spiritual joy was increased as new believers made decisions to follow the teaching of Jesus the Messiah.

Philippians 4:4 reads, 'Rejoice in the Lord always: and again I say, Rejoice."

The Apostle James rejoiced in the Lord always regardless of the circumstance. God is in control of all things and we are simply responsible for being obedient to His word, loving our neighbor, and praising and thanking Him for all blessings.

The Apostle James was part of the inner circle of Apostles and was under Jesus' teaching for three years, was present during the raising of Jairus' daughter, was in the Garden of Gethsemane with Jesus, and was present to see Jesus after the Resurrection. The Apostle James spoke with authority, with complete confidence, and with the power of the Holy Spirit. The Apostle James was filled by the Holy Spirit and experienced great spiritual joy.

Acts 12:1–3 reads, "Now about that time Herod the king stretched forth his hands to vex certain of the church. And he killed James the brother of John with the sword. And because he saw it pleased the Jews, he proceeded further to take Peter also. (Then were the days of unleavened bread.)"

The Apostle James and the early church were at this time (44AD) hated by the Jews and the chief priests, but the Apostle James continued to preach without fear the teachings of the Jesus the Messiah.

The Apostle James joy was not tied to this earth and its possessions, prestige, success, or reputation. He was a vessel filled with the Holy Spirit and all the spiritual joy James experienced came from the knowledge that the souls that were saved would experience eternity with their Lord and Savior. The rejoicing in heaven is beyond our comprehension.

The Apostle John (the beloved disciple) was an Apostle whose life was centered on his love for His Lord and Savior and his love for his neighbor.

1 John 1:4 reads, "And these things write we unto you, that your joy may be full."

John was sharing his personal experience of knowing his Lord and Savior and the joy that it brought him each day. John's joy was due to the fact his entire life was centered on God and his relationship with God. Consequently, his joy was not affected by circumstances or by the increase or decrease of possessions, prestige, reputation, or any other earthly pleasure. His joy was directly related to having the Holy Spirit fill him each day with joy as he praised and thanked God for his many blessings and continued to minister to God's people and the church.

Today the world and man is driven by expectations and how to achieve the next goal of wealth, possession, or position. The Apostle John and the other Apostles achieved spiritual joy by furthering the gospel and building the church. Our joy is also achieved by furthering the gospel and seeing how God's kingdom is expanded with each new soul.

Luke 15:4–7 reads, "What man of you, having a hundred sheep, if he lose one of them, doth not leave the ninety and nine in the in wilderness, and go after that which is lost, until he find it? And when he hath found it, he layeth it on his shoulders, rejoicing. And when he cometh home, he calleth together his friends and neighbors, saying unto them, rejoice with me; for I have found my sheep which was lost. I say unto you, that likewise joy shall be in heaven over one sinner that repenteth, more than over ninety and nine just persons, which need no repentance."

Man is God's creation and is of more value then we can comprehend. The purpose of the church is to care for and nourish the souls that attend and to search for those that are lost. Our churches should be focused on the conversion of those that have not made the decision to follow Jesus' teachings. Our church services should be filled with testimonies of those that have surrendered their life to Christ and have made a change in their life. The members of the church need to be experiencing spiritual joy along with those in heaven as testimonies are told of the life that has been changed. We were created for the purpose of praising God for his unbelievable gifts and blessings.

PRINCE OF PEACE

God promises the believer that He is watching over them, protecting them, and providing peace that we cannot explain.

Philippians 4:6–7 reads, "Be careful for nothing; but in everything by prayer and supplication with thanksgiving let your requests be made known unto God. And the peace of God, which passeth all understanding, shall keep your hearts and minds through Christ Jesus."

God is in control and there is no reason to worry. It is the believers' responsibility to bring all of our concerns to in God prayer. And, to bring all of our prayers of concerns with thanksgiving for the blessings we have

Application

received. It is important that we realize all that we are or ever will be is from God's love, mercy, and grace.

Moses knew of God's peace and how God is in control and how He provides new paths as old ones are closed.

Exodus 14:13-14 reads, "And Moses said unto the people, Fear ye not, stand still, and see the salvation of the Lord, which he will show to you today: for the Egyptians whom ye have seen today, ye shall see them again no more for ever. The Lord shall fight for you, and ye shall hold your peace."

We are to stand still and be quiet and wait for the Lord to provide direction. Our minds and thoughts should be focused on all of God's blessings, how He has comforted us, and how He has been faithful in so many ways and for so many years. From the beginning of time God has been there to love us and care for us.

Exodus 33:11 reads, "And the lord spake unto Moses face to face, as a man speaketh unto a friend. And he turns again into the camp: but his servant Joshua, the son of Nun, a young man, departed not out of the tabernacle."

Exodus 33:14 reads, "And he said, My presence shall go with thee, and I will give thee rest."

God spoke with Moses as a friend speaks to a friend and God promised that He would be with Moses and give him rest. Moses found grace and peace with the Lord and God would call him by name. God's divine presence and mighty majesty carried Moses to unfold great miracles to be accomplished for the Israelites.

Elijah was also given peace and comfort from God.

1 Kings 19:7 reads, "And the angel of the lord came again the second time, and touched him, and said, Arise and eat; because the journey is too great for thee."

God provided Elijah with nourishment and rest that would sustain him for a long and difficult journey through the desert. God was aware of Elijah's physical condition; the dangers he faced, and was ensuring that Elijah would be successful in unfolding God's plan and miracles.

God is continually providing protection and nourishment for those that follow His direction. We need to take every opportunity to thank God for His nourishment, protection, and unwavering faithfulness.

2 Kings 2:11 reads, "And it came to pass, as they still went on, and talked, that, behold, there appeared a chariot of fire, and horses of fire, and parted them both asunder; and Elijah went up by a whirlwind into heaven."

God was pleased with Elijah and collected him from this earth with a mighty display of His power. Elijah did not experience death and he was taken directly into God's presence. No army, no force can compare with God's power and might. Elijah was placed under great pressure and fear for being obedient to God's will. God responded by placing Elijah in heaven where he experienced complete peace and joy.

We need to reminder that we may experience difficult times, but our journey ends in complete peace with our Creator and Lord for eternity.

The Apostle Peter continually reminded the church that peace and grace would increase as the knowledge of Jesus Christ increased.

2 Peter 1:1-2 reads, "Simon Peter, a servant and an Apostle of Jesus Christ, to them that have obtained like precious faith with us through the righteousness of God and our Savior Jesus Christ. Grace and peace be multiplied unto you through the knowledge of God, and of Jesus our Lord."

We are to be fully engaged in taking advantage of our personal relationship with our Creator to experience the full impact of His peace and grace in our daily life. His peace and grace gives the knowledge to break free from the world and all of its evil desires and lusts. The world and it's obsession with wealth is extremely dangerous and will cause men to kill, steal, and destroy entire families. In some ways, the desire for wealth is like an addictive drug that will take control of every decision. This addiction will dictate standards for ethics, morals, and how men view his neighbor.

Romans 5:1-2 reads, "Therefore being justified by faith, we have peace with God through our Lord Jesus Christ. By whom also we have access by faith into this grace wherein we stand, and rejoice in hope of the glory of God."

We have been justified by our faith in the Lord Jesus Christ. Jesus Christ paid the price for us to enjoy the great peace that is available to all that have faith. As we travel through this journey of life we need to rejoice in all of God's blessings and rest in the peace that is beyond our understanding.

1 Peter 5:6-7 reads, "Humble yourselves therefore under the mighty hand of God, that he may exalt you in due time. Casting all your cares upon him; for he careth for you."

Our life has been turned over to God and His will. We wait and act in complete humility and prayer looking and listening for His direction and will for our life. We need to remember all those who have been martyred, those that have sacrificed everything, and the ultimate gift of God's only

Application

Son. We need to approach our Savior and Lord on our knees in complete humility.

The Holy Spirit is part of the Trinity and at the same time a separate entity within the same Deity. He is also called the great Comforter because of its ability to provide peace to people when they are under severe conflict, pain, and suffering. The peace that is provided by the Holy Spirit is a very unique peace that only the Holy Spirit is able to provide.

John 26–27 reads, "But the Comforter, which is the Holy Ghost, whom the Father will send in my name, he shall teach you all things, and bring all things to your remembrance, whatsoever I have said unto you. Peace I leave with you, my peace I give unto you: not as the world giveth, give I unto you. Let not your heart be troubled, neither let it be afraid."

The believer receives the glorious gift of the Holy Spirit when a decision is made and a confession of faith is declared through baptism. This is the same Holy Spirit that Peter received at Pentecost that allowed him to preach with such conviction that over 3,000 were baptized and converted to following Jesus' teachings. Most believers do not realize the power of the Holy Spirit within their life. The believer that is obedient to God's commands, has placed their full faith in our loving God, and is thankful for all of God's blessings will experience the peace of the Holy Spirit. The Holy Spirit is able to provide many blessings, such as confidence, the appropriate words in a difficult situation, love, compassion, and awareness of others situations, open opportunities that would not otherwise be available, and bringing people into your life for support and perspective. These are just a few of the blessings associated with living a life that allows the Holy Spirit to take up residence within your life and gives you God's peace.

The Apostle James was part of the inner circle of Jesus' Apostles and was present during many of Jesus' miracles. He was at the Garden of Gethsemane and saw Jesus as He prayed and went through the overwhelming sorrow as He approached death. The Apostle James as the other Apostles at Pentecost received the Holy Spirit and became Apostles of great faith. This glorious Apostle named as the (Son of Thunder) was executed by King Herod Agrippa because of his message that Jesus was the Messiah. It is believed that The Apostle James travels included Spain where he established the Christian Church. After his execution it is believed his body was shipped back to Spain.

The Apostle James, as were all believers, reconciled by Jesus Christ in His Crucifixion and will experience His peace for eternity.

Colossians 1:20 reads, "And, having made peace through the blood of his cross, by him to reconcile all things unto himself: by him, I say, whether they be things in earth, or things in heaven."

God's peace that was given to sinful man was only possible because of Jesus' sacrifice and His blood that was shed on the cross. The believer receives this peace daily because of the Holy Spirit's continual intercession for us as we struggle with daily challenges due to our weaknesses and temptations. This peace is God's peace and cannot be explained by man.

Psalm 139:1-6 reads, "O Lord thou hast searched me, and know me. Thou knowest my downsitting, and mine upraising; thou understandest my thoughts afar off. Thou compassest my path and my lying down, and art acquainted with all my ways. For there is not a word in my tongue, but, lo, O Lord, Thou hast beset me behind and before, and laid thine hand upon me. Such knowledge is too wonderful for me; it is high, I cannot attain unto it."

As believers we place our complete trust in God, we place Him at the center of our life, and wait patiently under His peace for His direction. Only God knows the true way for our life and we need to surrender to His direction. His path for our lives has been prepared and we need walk under his protection.

The Apostle James was filled with the peace of the Holy Spirit as he spoke of Jesus and the fact that He was the Messiah. Some believe he sang as he was lead to his execution.

The Apostle John was a man of God's love and peace.

John 20:19-22 reads, "Then the same day at evening, being the first day of the week, when the doors were shut where the disciples were assembled for fear of the Jews, came Jesus and stood in the midst, and saith unto them, Peace be unto you. And when he had so said, he showed unto them his hands and his side. Then were the disciples glad, when they saw the Lord. Then said Jesus to them again, Peace be unto you: as my Father hath sent me, even so send I you. And when he had said this, he breathed on them, and saith unto them, Receive ye the Holy Ghost."

The Apostle John and others were meeting behind locked doors in fear not knowing if they would be the next to be arrested and possibly crucified. The miraculous appearance of Jesus in this room gave the disciples the peace that passes all understanding. This type of peace erased all doubt, established confidence, and fulfilled their faith. They were in fact vessels that were now prepared to receive the Holy Spirit. At this point, the Holy Spirit was able to transform each of disciples and work with them individually to carry out God's plan. At some time later, all believers were baptized by the Holy Spirit at Pentecost and were sent out speaking many different languages.

The Apostle John understood the meaning of peace and spoke of peace to the churches he ministered.

John 16:33 reads, "These things I have spoken unto you, that in me ye might have peace. In the world ye shall have tribulation: but be of good cheer; I have overcome the world."

Believers have made a decision to follow Jesus Christ and His teaching and are therefore walking with the Holy Spirit in God's plan. However, believers are still in this world and pressured by Satan and his demons. The Apostle John in this verse was reminding these believers to be at peace in knowing God is control and he has beaten evil at every step. As believers we are to rest in God's grace knowing our sins were forgiven by the sacrifice of God's only Son.

As natural men we have many frailties and a fallen nature that invades our daily life with many distractions that are destructive to living a Christ centered life.

John 14:27 reads, "Peace I leave with you, my peace I give unto you: not as the world giveth, give I unto you. Let not your heart be troubled, neither let it be afraid."

We are bombarded each day by a world that has a set of morals and ethics that are based on pleasure, pride of life, and greed. As our society continues to crumble, with no moral or ethical guide, our leadership does not provide any type of direction for reversing a path to civil anarchy. The lack of respect for another person, the sense of entitlement, and the act of killing another person for no reason is the result of a society without values or morals.

The peace that a believer receives is not from the world or from anything that is related to the world. Peace from God is not related to wealth, pleasure, or any other aspect of worldly living. A believer's peace comes from knowing that they are living in God's will, they have eternal security, God will supply for their needs, and God will direct them as to which path to follow.

A natural man (e.g., carnal man, fallen man) is a man that completely dependent on physical things and unable to receive and preserve spiritual blessings from the Holy Spirit. A natural man is completely possessed by physical desires, senses of pleasures, taste, touch, emotions, pride of life, and ego. He is controlled by his eyes and heart as he lusts for evil, for status, and wealth.

1 Corinthians 2:14 reads, "But the natural man received not the things of the spirit of God: for they are foolishness unto him: neither can he know them, because they are spiritually discerned."

A natural man takes on many of the characteristics of Satan and his demons as he goes through life self absorbed and dispensing evil to those that get in his way. The soul and spirit of the natural man escapes into a deep hibernation and can only be awaken by the Holy Spirit.

The spiritual man knows the voice of the Lord and is able to experience peace knowing he is in God's will.

John 10:3–5 reads, "To him the porter openeth; and the sheep hear his voice: and he calleth his own sheep by name, and leadeth them out. And when he putteth forth his own sheep, he goeth before them, and the sheep follow him: for they know his voice. And a stranger will they not follow, but will fee from him: for they know not the voice of strangers."

God calls each individual by name and leads them through their life. God's leading is obvious when people look back over their life and see how God has open doors, changed events, and used others to lead or change their attitudes.

To hear or grow in our faith we need to realize that the goals and values of the world are not God's goals and values. His direction for our life may not be what we want for our life. And, to hear God's voice requires us to change how we think and to train our minds to close out the noise of the world and to allow His Spirit to take control of our thoughts. God's speaks to each of us throughout each day.

John 4:24 reads, "God is a Spirit: and they that worship him must worship him in spirit and in truth."

The Holy Spirit does commune with the spiritual man in ways that are not understood by the natural man. The Holy Spirit acts as a conduit between man and God as He creates ideas and impressions within a spiritual man's spirit. These thoughts and impressions are given frequently throughout each day to man for developing ideas and impressions. The gift of the Holy Spirit to a spiritual man brings great peace, joy, and allows him to rejoice in the knowledge he is in God's will. A spiritual man's life has purpose and that purpose is following God's direction.

The natural man worships his possessions and all other things and has stopped his soul and spirit from functioning. Sin and Satan has blinded the natural man and caused him to consider worshiping God as foolishness.

1 Kings 19:12 reads, "And after the earthquake a fire, but the Lord was not in the fire: and after the fire a still small voice."

Elijah, a spiritual man, was able to hear this still small voice. Elijah's heart and mind knew God's voice and was able to recognize that it was God speaking to him. It is when we are silent and separated from the world our spirit begins to hear and recognize God's thoughts and impressions. The thoughts we receive from our spirit are not like most thoughts. They are like whispers that are easily forgotten in a manner of minutes. In most cases they need to be written down before they are lost.

Proverbs 24:3-4 reads, "Through wisdom is a house builded; and by understanding it, is established. And by knowledge shall the chambers be filled with all precious and pleasant riches."

Every person has a spirit and soul; however few people understand it or know how to care for it. The natural man has a mind that is completely consumed by thoughts and ideas based on the world's values and ethics. In most cases any thought of a spiritual nature is immediately discarded. The natural man's mind is at war with the spiritual and will drown out any spiritual thought or distract the mind with other thoughts. Controlling your thoughts or selecting thoughts is difficult and requires God's strength and direction.

Isaiah 11:2 reads, "And the spirit of the Lord shall rest upon him, the spirit of wisdom and understanding, the spirit of counsel and might, the spirit of knowledge and the fear of the Lord."

Most people need to set aside some time each day to be at peace with God's word and allow the Holy Spirit to commune with our spirit. In prayer we praise His name, thank Him for the gift of His son and His many daily blessings, ask for forgiveness for our many sins, and submit our requests and concerns. We need to be at rest to allow our spirit and mind to focus on what is really a priority.

LONGSUFFERING

God selected Moses, Elijah, Peter, James, and John because they lived and acted knowing God's will and timing and not man's will and timing. God's plan for mankind and how He unfolds His plan is only known to God.

Generally, we are able to see God's plans as we look back over many years. When we come to the realization and understanding that only God is in control and we need to place all of our trust in Him that we come to a place of peace.

We are all placed in situations where we need to be patient and endure difficulties. As we go through these circumstances we begin to develop strength and are better able to endure persecution. The growing in faith and communing with the Holy Spirit is directly related to developing patience and endurance in difficult situations. It is extremely important that we allow the Holy Spirit to take control in difficult situations. The Holy Spirit is able to carry us through difficult times and to provide a resting place for our emotions and mind.

Ephesians 3:10-15, "To the intent that now unto the principalities and powers in heavenly places might be know by the church the manifold wisdom of God. According to the eternal purpose which be purposed in Christ Jesus our Lord: In whom we have boldness and access with confidence by the faith of him. Wherefore I desire that ye faint not at my tribulations for you, which is your glory. For this cause I bow my knees unto the Father of our Lord Jesus Christ. Of whom the whole family in heaven and earth is named."

We are a member of a family of believers that number in the millions that are both in heaven and on earth. All of these members have derived their faith from God our Creator and He now counts each one of us as His own.

The Jewish people suffered greatly for hundreds of years as slaves under the barbaric rule of the Egyptians until God called Moses to lead them to the Promised Land. Even then the Jewish people suffered as they wandered the desert for 40 years because of lack of faith and the sin of building pagan gods. God strengthened Moses and gave Moses the endurance to experience the longsuffering of leading over 600,000 people through the desert.

Exodus 34:5-6 reads, "And the Lord descended in the cloud. And stood with him there, and proclaimed the name of the Lord. And the Lord passed by before him, and proclaimed, The Lord, The Lord God, merciful and gracious, long-suffering, and abundant in goodness and truth."

God is merciful and patient with us as we struggle with sin in a world that is lost in pride of life, distorted values, and the refusal to recognize all of God's blessings.

Application

Psalm 103:7–14 reads, "He made known his ways unto Moses, his acts unto the children of Israel. The Lord is merciful and gracious, slow to anger, and plenteous in mercy. He will not always chide: neither will he keep his anger forever. He hath not dealt with us after our sins, nor rewarded us according to our iniquities. For as the heavens is high above the earth, so great is his mercy toward them that fear him. As far as the east is from the west, so far hath he removed our transgressions from us. Like as a father pitieth his children, so the Lord pitieth them that fear him. For he knoweth our frame; he remembereth that we are dust."

God was slow to anger with both Moses and the Israelites; he is merciful, patient, and gives us time to repent of our sins. We need to approach our Lord and Savior with a contrite heart, with weeping, asking for forgiveness and asking for His mercy.

Elijah was a man who suffered greatly under the rule of King Ahab and Jezebel for not worshiping the pagan god Baal. King Ahab and Jezebel were extremely wicked rulers that were under the influence of Satan that forced all people to worship Baal and other pagan gods. This worship included many temple prostitutes and many other unspeakable acts of human degradation.

Mark 7:21–23 reads, "For from within, out of the heart of men, proceed evil thoughts, adulteries, fornication, murders. Thefts, covetousness, wickedness, deceit, lasciviousness, an evil eye, blasphemy, pride, foolishness: All these evil things come from within, and defile the man."

The natural man is full of evil and it is apparent in the words he uses, the thoughts he entertains, and the actions he takes. However, those that are believers are given the Holy Spirit that leads and instructs man in ways that are pleasing to God. We live in a world that is lost in sin and suffering and we experience that suffering as Christ experienced that suffering. However, we need to remember that we are only here for a short time and the suffering we encounter is insignificant compared to the glory that we will experience as God pores out His never ending love upon us. All of creation will bear the pain of a new birth when Christ returns to claim his own.

Revelation 21:1–4, reads, "And I saw a new heaven and a new earth, for the first heaven and the first earth were passed away: and there was no more sea. And I John saw the holy city, new Jerusalem, coming down from God out of heaven, prepared as a bride adorned for her husband. And I heard a great voice out of heaven saying, Behold the tabernacle of God is with men, and he will dwell with them, and they shall be his people, and

God himself shall be with them, and be their God. And God shall wipe away all tears from their eyes; and there shall be no more death, neither sorrow, nor crying, neither shall there be any more pain: for the former things are passed away."

Elijah was completely dependent on God for his entire life. He obeyed God when he approached King Ahab and prophesied a drought that would last for three years. We need to be obedient to God's direction and wait patiently for the next door to be opened. We all go through difficult times and we all are subject to tests. However, the only way to grow in faith and to be redeemed out of this world is to go through suffering and tests. We can all rest in the knowledge that God's love will only allow those suffering and trials in our life that is for our benefit.

Troubling events and problems affect all of mankind in some way. For some, these events have a dramatic impact on their life, whereas others these same events have different or little impact. The believer through their faith has the power and grace of the Holy Spirit in their life and can at any time request His peace in prayer. God deals with each individual in ways that addresses his or her faith.

God took Elijah out of complete obscurity and used him to turn thousands of people from pagan worship to the worship of the one and true God. As Moses, Elijah experienced the power and grace of God Our Father. He also experienced the long-suffering as Jesus Christ did in being obedient to God and following His direction.

Romans 11:33 reads, "O the depth of the riches both of the wisdom and knowledge of god! How unsearchable are his judgments, and his ways past finding out."

God's paths and ways are never ending and are available for all believers to search and experience His blessings.

The Apostle Peter did not consider himself or the followers of Jesus Christ to be residents of this world. Therefore they would not have the same values and morals of the natural man. And, because of these differences they would suffer greatly from many different sources.

1 Peter 1:1 reads, "Peter, an apostle of Jesus Christ, to the strangers scattered throughout Pontus, Galatia, Cappadocia, Asia, and Bithynia."

When we suffer as believers we are being identified with the suffering of Jesus on the cross. Suffering provides a way for us to prove our faith in our Lord and Savior.

Application

Peter had firsthand knowledge of the suffering of Jesus the Christ as Christ hung on the cross to be a sacrifice for all the sins of mankind.

1 Peter 1:22–25 reads, "Seeing ye have purified your soul in obeying the truth through the Spirit unto unfeigned love of the brethren, see that ye love one another with a pure heart fervently. Being born again not of corruptible seed, but of incorruptible, by the word of God, which liveth and abideth for ever. For ALL FLESH IS AS GRASS, AND ALL THE GLORY OF MAN AS THE FLOWERS OF GLASS. THE GRASS WITHERETH, AND THE FLOWERS THEREOF FALLETH AWAY: But the word of the Lord ENDURETH FOR EVER. And this is the word which by the gospel is preached unto you."

As we live through suffering our focus as believers is to purify our souls as we obey God's commands to love the Lord with all our heart and to love your neighbor as our self. We long for the word of God because it provides nourishment for our souls and allows us access to His glory.

1 Peter 4:12–14 reads, "Beloved think it not strange concerning the fiery trial which is to try you, as though some strange thing happen unto you. But rejoice inasmuch as ye are partakers of Christ's suffering; that, when his glory shall be revealed, ye may be glad also with exceeding joy. If ye be reproached for the name of Christ, happy are ye; for the spirit of glory and of God resteth upon you: on their part he is evil spoken of, but on your part he is glorified."

If you suffer because you are a believer you will be blessed and identified with the glory of God. Suffering for Christ is a reason for rejoicing because it identifies the believer with Christ. Sharing the suffering of Christ allows a believer to take part in His glory, to commune in joy with the Holy Spirit, and is a privilege.

The Apostle Peter considered the long-suffering of the believer as a process one goes through to refine their faith. A believer continues to deal with sin on a daily basis and may fail and may be disciplined.

1 Peter 4:19 reads, "Wherefore let them that suffer according to the will of God commit the keeping of their souls to him in well doing, as unto a faithful Creator."

As believers we continue to live a holy life by entrusting our souls to our Creator who judges justly and indentifies himself with the faithful. Just as Christ entrusted Himself to the Father, so do we need to entrust our souls to our Lord and Savior.

1 Peter 3:12 reads, "FOR THE EYES OF THE LORD ARE OVER THE RIGHTEOUS, AND HIS EARS ARE OPEN UNTO THEIR PRAYERS: BUT THE FACE OF THE LORD IS AGAINST THEM THAT DO EVIL."

The Apostle Peter reminded his followers that obedience to God's word was the best defense against unjust punishment and persecution. Believers are able to overcome fear by being sanctified in God's word.

There is little known about The Apostle James (the greater) the son of Zebedee and Salome, and older brother of the Apostle John. He was one of the early Apostles who spread the Gospel across Israel and the Roman kingdom. It is believed he travel to Spain where he ministered for many for years and later returned to Jerusalem where he was martyred. The Apostle James was a gifted speaker who delivered fiery messages that caught the attention of the temple priests. During this early time period it is estimated that over 2,000 followers were subject to long-suffering and were martyred for their faith. We need to remember many people actually saw Jesus after the Resurrection and were able to see His wounds from the Crucifixion. For those people who actually saw Jesus, it was a fact that Jesus was God and their Messiah. Jesus left no doubt in the minds of the temple priest that he claimed to be God and was guilty of the crime of blasphemy. Any follower or Apostle of Jesus would also be also guilty of this crime and subject to Roman rule. However, any person that witnessed the Crucifixion and Resurrection of Jesus would know the truth that Jesus was God and would hold fast to their faith regardless of the danger or risk of death.

1 Corinthians 13:4–5 reads, "Charity suffereth long, and is kind; charity envieth not; charity vaunteth not itself, is not puffed up. Doth not behave itself unseemly, seeketh not her own, is not easily provoked, thinketh no evil."

A believer's long-suffering involves being patience and not to strike back. Long-suffering also involves showing love, kindness, and goodness. Our Lord is slow to anger and great in mercy. Our faith is built upon long-suffering, patience, and trusting God to provide us with our needs. There are many who can testify of living a life where they can detail where God has created opportunities where there was no hope.

Isaiah 40:31 reads, "But they that wait upon the Lord shall renew their strength; they shall mount up with wings as eagles; they shall run, and not be weary; and they shall walk, and not faint."

We as believers need to be patience and long-suffering as we place our trust in God's leading. We are completely dependent on the Holy Spirit

Application

for wisdom and understanding as we present our requests in prayer and thanksgiving. We wait on God for He knows the best time for when we will be ready and when events are to fall into place.

Ephesians 4:1-3 reads, "I therefore, the prisoner of the Lord, beseech you that ye walk worthy of the vocation wherewith ye are called. With all lowliness and meekness, with long-sufffering, forbearing one another in love; Endeavoring to keep the unity of the spirit in the bond of peace."

A believer's daily walk is in complete humility and in complete obedience to God. One that is controlled by God is angry only at the right time and only for the right reason. Jesus became angry when the temple was being used by thieves to steal from the poor.

The Apostle John was the younger brother of James and a son of Zebedee and Salome. The Apostle John had a home in Jerusalem and it is believed that is where Mary the mother Jesus lived after the Crucifixion. The Apostle John was persecuted and beaten as the other Apostle throughout his life.

Revelations 1:9-11 reads, "I John who also am your brother, and companion in tribulation, and in the kingdom and patience of Jesus Christ, was in the isle that is called Patmos, for the word of God, and for the testimony of Jesus Christ. I was in the spirit on the Lord's day, and heard behind the me a great voice, as of a trumpet. Saying, I am Alpha and Omega, the first and the last: and, What thou seest, write in a book, and send it unto the seven churches which are in Asia; unto Ephesus, and unto Smyrna, and unto Pergamos, and unto Thyatira, and unto Sardis, and unto Philadelphia, and unto Laodicea."

The Apostle John moved to Ephesus and later in his ministry he was imprisoned and sent to the island of Patmos for preaching the word of God and testifying as a witness to Jesus' Crucifixion and Resurrection. On Patmos, the Apostle John was living and working in a mining community. In spite of being imprisoned and subject to hard labor the Apostle John maintained his close relationship with his Lord and Savior. John was under the protection and strength of God that allowed him to experience the long-suffering and the patience to place all his trust in God.

We all go through difficult times of long-suffering where we need to develop patience and realize we need to place all of trust in our Lord and Savior. God is involved in virtually every aspect of our life. God is omniscient, omnipotent, and omnipresent. God knows all things, he knows our thoughts and our words before your speak. God has unlimited power, He created the heaven and earth. God is always present; he is present in our thoughts. Few people have a good understanding of our personal relationship with our Lord and Savior. Their prayers are generally limited and are restricted to only a few times during the day.

Hebrews 13:5 reads, "Let your conversion be without covetousness; and be content with such things as ye have for he hath said, I WILL NEVER LEAVE THEE, NOR FORSAKE THEE."

God is with us throughout each day and wants a personal relationship with Him as we encounter challenges and distractions. Our first response to all challenges is to first turn them over to God for His direction and power. God is our Lord and Savior, our friend and comforter and He will answer our prayers in His time in a way that is best for us. The Holy Spirit will comfort our spirits and provide thoughts and ideas as to how to resolve problems.

Colossians 3:23 reads, "And whatsoever ye do, do it hearty, as to the Lord, and not unto man."

As believers we work using all of our skills and talents to provide the best possible service or product. God has blessed us with work that we may glorify Him so that we may be a good testimony to others. A worker that follows directions, shows genuine concern, and is able to exceed expectations is valued by all.

KINDNESS

Moses was a kind and humble shepherd who spent 40 years of his life caring for his father-in-law's sheep in the wilderness. God found Moses in the desert caring for sheep and took him and molded him into one of the world's greatest leaders. It was because of Moses' humility and kindness that God was able to mold him into a great leader. His life started from the humblest of beginnings when his mother placed him in small ark and allowed the river Nile and God to take control and deliver his small basket before the eyes of the Pharaohs' daughter who adopted him and cared for him.

Numbers 12:3 reads, "Now the man Moses was very meek, above all the men which were upon the face of the earth."

Moses was a common man who worked as a Shepherd caring for sheep each day with only a rod or stick to protect the sheep from dangers such as wolves and other wild animals. He felt he did not have the skills or abilities to carry out God's commands.

Application

Exodus 4:10 reads, "And Moses said unto the Lord, O my Lord, I am not eloquent, neither heretofore, nor since thou hast spoken unto thy servant: but I am slow of speech, and of a slow tongue."

Moses was not confident in his ability to speak clearly or have the ability to convince others to follow his direction. He felt at the age of 80 there were others much better equipped to fill the position. God had to remind him that God was his Creator and he will make him into an eloquent speaker, a dynamitic speaker, and a charismatic speaker. Moses was allowing his fears to control him and to convince him that he could not be a leader. Moses had to learn to let go of his fears and trust God to give him the words to speak and trust God to correct his slow speak issue. We are all guilty of hanging onto excuses for not trusting God. We measure everything on the basis of a short term payback and we forget that God's time table may expand generations.

Proverbs 3:5–7 reads, "Trust in the Lord with all thine heart; and lean not unto thine own understanding. In all thy ways acknowledge him, and he shall direct thy paths. Be not wise in thine own eyes: fear the lord, and depart from evil."

Moses knew that trusting in one's own abilities and knowledge was not enough to achieve joy and fill the void for self fulfillment. It is only when one is filled by the Holy Spirit that the void is filled and one can rest in the knowledge of eternal salvation.

The natural man knows the meaning of fear and in most cases realizes its value. However, the natural man has no concept of the power of God and can only see the physical. It was only when Moses finally submitted to God's leading that God began his work of transforming Moses.

Moses was an extremely humble and kind man. His heart was full with the love for the Jewish people and had great sorrow for their bondage and severe treatment. Moses was an advocate for the Jewish people and asked God not to destroy them for their many sins and failures to keep God's commands.

Isaiah 57:15 reads, "For thus saith the high and lofty One that inhabiteth eternity, whose name is Holy; I dwell in the high and holy place, with him also that is of a contrite and humble spirit, and to revive the spirit of the humble, and to revive the heart of the contrite ones."

God considers a humble and contrite heart as the greatest virtue within His creation, man. God provided man with His word and revealed to him His truth to follow with a humble and contrite heart.

Witnesses to a Great Miracle

Elijah was a little known priest and prophet who lived off the land and donations. Like Moses, God found Elijah in the wilderness with few possessions. God was able to use both Moses and Elijah because of their humility, kindness, goodness, and openness to God's spirit and direction.

God approached Elijah during a period in time when Israel and its people were morally bankrupt. They had sunken to great social depths during a time when the rulers were very corrupt and people were suffering from hunger and poverty.

God directed Elijah to go to King Ahab to condemn his decree that all should worship Baal and other pagan gods. Because of this decree Elijah also prophesied that a drought would occur and would last for three years. Elijah feared for his life after making this prophecy and went into hiding. Eventually God directed Elijah to go to the home of a poor widow.

1 Kings 17:10-14 reads, "So he arose and went to Zarephath. And when he came to the gate of the city, behold, the widow woman was there gathering of sticks: and he called to her, and said, Fetch me, I pray thee, a little water in a vessel, that I may drink. And as she was going to fetch it, he called to her, and said, Bring me, I pray thee, a morsel of bread in thine hand. And she said, As the Lord the God liveth, I have not a cake, but a handful of meal in a barrel, and a little oil in a cruse: and, behold , I am gathering two sticks, that I may go in and dress it for me and my son, that we may eat it, and die. And Elijah said unto her, Fear not: go and do as thou hast said, but make me thereof a little cake first, and bring it unto me, and after make for thee and thy son. For thus saith the Lord God of Israel. The barrel of meal shall not waste, neither shall the cruse of oil fail, until the day that the Lord sendeth rain upon the earth."

God knew that that the widow and her son were starving and that Elijah was also starving. God knew that this widow was about to kill herself and her son. God through his mercy, kindness and goodness directed Elijah to go Zarpehath and to meet this widow and ask for food. Elijah recognized the plight of this widow and son and through God's mercy he asked her not to fear and to prepare a cake for him and herself and her son. The widow followed Elijah's directions and put her life in his hands.

As believers it is critical that we follow God's direction and allow His love, mercy and kindness flow through us to those who are waiting for a miracle. As believers our lives are woven as a fine tapestry all working together to form the master piece of God's creation.

Application

The natural or fallen man's morals or ethics is primarily based on pleasure or what feels good. If it feels good it must be right. There is no reference to the Bible or church teachings. Consequently, greed, pride, and pleasure take control of most of the attitudes, emotions, and decisions made by the natural man.

God's word and commands in many cases are the complete opposite of what the world considers to be appropriate. One of the most repeated commands in the Bible is to love your neighbor. This one command in many cases is probably one of the most forgotten or ignored commands by the world. As believers we are representatives of God's message that He loved all people and gave His only Son that we may spend eternity with Him. A believer has access to God's power, mercy and grace that can be ignited by prayer. Praying for a neighbor is in most cases the greatest gift or most effective way of making a difference in a neighbor's life.

1 Samuel 16:7 reads, "But the Lord said unto Samuel, Look not on his countenance, or on height of his stature; because I have refused him: for the Lord seeth not as man seeth; for man looketh on the outward appearance, but the Lord looketh on the heart."

The world values a man by the number of his possessions, wealth, and his position within society. Elijah had no possessions, no wealth, and no position. However, God used Elijah to transform Israel from a country lost in sin to a country that worshiped the one true and only God. God values man by the condition of his heart and the kindness, mercy, and love that he shows to his neighbor.

The Apostle James was one of the older Apostles and in some ways more prepared to accept the task of following Jesus and learning from His teaching. When Jesus asked James to follow him, James did not hesitate to leave his fishing boat. James was enthusiastic and his preaching reflected that enthusiasm as he spoke without fear and challenged the traditional beliefs. James knew the risks and he knew the message of the cross and he was willing to drink from the cup that would lead to his death 14 years later.

Titus 3:4–5 reads, "But after that the kindness and love of God our Savior toward man appeared. Not by works of righteousness which we have done, but according to his mercy he saved us, by the washing of regeneratation, and renewing of the Holy Spirit."

The Apostle James' heart was prepared to follow Jesus before Jesus asked him to follow. He was unique in knowing his purpose in life and knowing what kindness was.

The natural or fallen man is enslaved to pleasure, to self, and the lust of the flesh. God knew of the hurt, suffering and lack of hope in a world where man's heart was not filled with kindness for his fellow man. It was only God's mercy and kindness that broke Satan's shacks of sin, hatred of fellow man, and lust of the flesh. The Holy Spirit changes a man's heart to be obedient to God's word and to give hope where there is no hope, to change an attitude of resignation to an attitude of achievement, and to change hate to love for his neighbor.

The emotional and impetuous Peter was an Apostle who had great love for his Lord and Savior.

2 Peter 1:1–7 reads, "Simon Peter, a servant and an apostle of Jesus Christ, to them that have obtained like precious faith with us through the righteousness of God and our Savior Jesus Christ. Grace and peace be multiplied unto you through the knowledge of God, and of Jesus our Lord. According as his divine power hath given unto us all things that pertain unto life, and godliness, through the knowledge of him that hath called us to glory and virtue. Whereby are given unto us exceeding great and precious promises: that by these ye might be partakers of the divine nature, having escaped the corruption that is in the world through lust. And beside this, giving all diligence, add to your faith virtue, and to virtue knowledge. And to knowledge temperance; and to temperance patience; and to patience godliness; And to godliness brotherly kindness; and to brotherly kindness charity."

The Apostle Peter understood the lifelong struggle of spiritual maturity that begins with faith that is based in the righteousness of God and our Savior Jesus the Christ. Faith opens the door to peace and spiritual knowledge. Spiritual knowledge allows for the understanding of God's truths with patience, self control, and without the world's corruption.

The Apostle Peter was also aware of those who were suffering and followed Jesus' example in showing mercy and kindness to those who were in need.

Acts 9:32–35 reads, "And it came to pass, as Peter passed throughout all quarters, he came down also to the saints which dwelt at Lydda. And there he found a certain man named Aeneas, which had kept his bed eight years, and was sick of the palsy. And Peter said unto him, Anneas, Jesus Christ maketh thee whole: arise, and make thy bed. And he arose immediately. And all that dwelt at Lydda and Saron saw him, and turned to the Lord."

Application

Peter called upon the name of Jesus and allowed the power of His spirit to flow through him to heal Aeneas of the palsy. This act of kindness and mercy had a profound effect on Lydda and Saron and the entire community returned to worshiping the one and true God.

The Apostle also traveled to Joppa where he healed a woman named Tabitha (Dorcas).

Acts 9:40 reads, "But Peter put them all forth, and kneeled down, and prayed; and turning him to the body said, Tabitha, arise. And she opened her eyes, and when she saw Peter, she sat up."

Tabitha (Dorcas) was a woman full of good works and a believer. Peter's heart was touched by the generosity of this woman and those that testified of her many works of kindness. God saw that this woman had provided great service to the church and prayed that she might continue so that others may receive the blessings of her service.

1 Peter 1:22 reads, "Seeing ye have purified your soul in obeying the truth through the spirit unto unfeigned love of the brethren, see that ye love one another with a pure heart fervently."

The message is clear. If you want to know God it is essential that you love your neighbors and show them kindness. Jesus also stated that others would be able to identify you as a believer because of your kindness to your neighbor. This one principle is extremely important for a believer to grow and develop a relationship with their Lord and Savior. Other issues that will prevent or block communion with the Holy Spirit are sinfulness, greed, selfishness, and the lack of compassion for the poor and those in need.

Acts 5:15–16 reads, "Insomuch that they brought forth the sick into the streets, and laid them on beds and couches, that at the least the shadow of Peter passing by might overshadow some of them. There came also a multitude out of the cities round about unto Jerusalem, bringing sick folks, and them which were vexed with unclean spirits: and they were healed every one."

Mark 16:15–18 reads, "And he said unto them, Go ye into the world, and preach the gospel to every creature. He that believeth and is baptized shall be saved; but he that believeth not shall be dammed. And these signs shall follow them that believe; In my name shall they cast out devils; they shall speak with new tongues; They shall take up serpents; and if they drink any deadly thing, it shall not hurt them; they shall lay hands on the sick, and they shall recover."

Witnesses to a Great Miracle

The Apostle Peter was given the divine power of God to heal those who were suffering from sickness and to cast out demons from those who were possessed. The Apostle Peter with the divine power and mercy of the Holy Spirit blessed many and revealed God's kindness and love for His creation.

The Apostle John was the youngest and lived the longest of the Apostles. The Apostle John's life was focused on being in the will of God and preaching the gospel of the kingdom of God and His return. He was beaten a number of times and spent time in prison for preaching the word of God.

John 7:38 reads, "He that believeth on me, as the scripture hath said, out of his belly shall flow rivers of living water."

The Apostle John had a profound relationship with Jesus and understood the importance of having the Holy Spirit direct his daily life. Jesus and the Holy Spirit transformed his personality, his values, and his heart to a man of great compassion and love for all of God's creation.

The Holy Spirit changed John the fisherman (the natural and fallen man) into a new creature. The Apostle John was a man who lived for the purpose of saving souls and revealing God's plan for all of mankind. The Holy Spirit convicted John of his natural man's flaws and filled those areas with kindness and compassion for all those in need.

Jesus knew and trusted the Apostle John with the care of his mother (Mary). Jesus recognized the depth of kindness and love of the Apostle John and entrusted him as the provider for the care of Mary.

1 John 4:7–8 reads, "Beloved let us love one another for love is of God; and every one that loveth is born of God, and knoweth God. He that loveth not knoweth not God; for God is love."

The Apostle John experienced the full meaning of love when he stood with Mary at the foot of the cross where Jesus the Christ gave His life for all. The love and kindness that is shared by each believer is the love and kindness from the Holy Spirit that indwells each believer.

The Apostle John was bold and direct in his writing and preaching in delivering the message of obeying God's commands and loving one another. This glorious Apostle continually spoke of God the Redeemer and the need to show charity for your neighbor. The Apostle John often explained that he who does not love his neighbor does not know God, for God is charity. He would also speak of obeying God's commands and avoid all sin to prove your love for God.

APPLICATION

1 John 4:20 reads, "If a man say, I love God, and hateth his brother, he is a liar: for he that loveth not his brother whom he hath seen , how can he love God whom he hath not seen?"

Loving God is following His commands, showing charity, willingness to sacrifice, and show kindness to your neighbor. A believer's faith provides victory over the world and its values and allows the believer to grow in faith.

The Apostle John reminded man that to maintain a close relationship with God he must place his desires for the things of the world and his selfish desires in its proper perspective. You cannot love the world or the things of the world and also love God. You cannot have two masters you will love one and hate the other.

SELF CONTROL

Moses had a unique childhood and had many advantages living in the Pharaoh's palace. During this time he grew in appreciation of his Jewish heritage and grew to love the Jewish people. He also grew in anger over the violent and brutal treatment the Jewish people were receiving under slavery.

Moses' anger took control over him when he was watching an Egyptian guard beat a Hebrew slave. In an uncontrollable rage Moses killed the Egyptian guard and buried the body in the sand. Moses was acting as a natural and fallen man that had allowed anger to control his entire being. Unfortunately, today there is epidemic of uncontrollable anger where the natural man will attack and kill their brothers and sisters for little or no reason.

Moses spent the next forty years in the desert herding sheep and considering his actions before God approached him to lead the Israelites out of Egypt. Moses again becomes angry when he returns after 40 days from Mount Sinai with the Ten Commandments. On his return he finds his brother Aaron and a golden calf he had made for the people to worship.

At this point God became angry and wanted to destroy all the people, but Moses intervened and pleaded that God would show His mercy for His people that were weak and desperately sinful. The anger shown by God and Moses was righteous anger.

Moses on another occasion became angry when God tells him to speak to a rock for water. He is under a great deal of pressure from the continual complaining of the Israelites and in anger he strikes the rock with his rod rather than speak to the rock as God commanded. Moses' anger in this situation had taken control over him and the result is disobedience to God. This anger, loss of self control, and disobedience resulted in Moses not being able to enter the Promised Land.

We have a cause and effect relationship with God. When we are in His will and obedient to his word we receive blessings. When we are trusting in ourselves and disobedient to his word we experience the consequences. This relationship is subject to God's will and timing.

2 Peter 3:8 reads, "But, beloved, be not ignorant of this one thing, that one day is with the lord as a thousand years, and a thousand years as one day."

A believer has a personal relationship with their Lord and that relationship involves the continual exchange between the physical and the spiritual. God deals with each individual on an individual basis and is continually encouraging and strengthening each individual to fulfill His purpose of ministering to all of His creation.

God dealt with Moses directly, corrected him, encouraged him, and built him into a great leader that led over 600,000 people through the wilderness for 40 years. A number of individuals became angry in the Bible. However, becoming angry and losing self control or holding on to bitterness for an extended period of time can have a devastating effect on entire families, friends, and neighbors. Words spoken in anger or words spoken without compassion are words that are not forgotten and can cause permanent damage in any relationship. We need to be in prayer each day asking for God's grace, power, and mercy as we struggle to control our thoughts, emotions, and words. As we struggle with sin each day we have Jesus Christ as our example as a man who lived a life without sin.

Elijah was a man that God could use to further His kingdom because his heart and soul were open and obedient to God's direction. God was able to accomplish great things through Elijah. God and Elijah were able to convert thousands of people from the worshiping of pagan gods to the worshiping the one true God. God used Elijah to destroy 450 pagan priest controlled by Jezebel. However, Jezebel was completely under the control of Satan and his demons and involved in many pagan rituals that included debauchery and other unspeakable sins.

1 Kings 19:4 reads, "But he himself went a day's journey into the wilderness, and came and sat down under a juniper tree: and he requested for himself that he might die, and said, It is enough; now, O Lord, take away my life; for I am not better than my fathers."

Application

Elijah had experienced great joy being in God's will and having great success, converting thousands of souls and then experienced great fear when he realized Jezebel wanted to kill him. It was more than he could handle and he was at the point of ending his life. He had lost self control and was falling into depression.

1 kings 19:7 reads, "And the angel of the Lord came again the second time, and touched him, and said, Arise and eat; because the journey is too great for thee."

In this case the angel of the Lord tells Elijah of another assignment and the need for him to think about getting prepared for the journey. As believers we need to be focused on the next assignment and getting prepared for the journey home. We also have the Holy Spirit that will comfort us when we are confused or in a difficult situation. We are complex individuals with many different challenges that only God can address and provide a solution.

Jesus Christ told the Apostle Peter that he would deny him three times. The Apostle Peter assured Jesus he would never deny him. However, the night when Jesus was arrested, beaten and taken for trial; Peter became extremely fearful and lost control of his emotions and denied that he knew Jesus three times. Peter was not prepared for the reality of the arrest and had slept rather then spent time in prayer and preparation as Jesus had requested.

1 Peter 5:8 reads, "Be sober, be vigilant; because your adversary the devil, as a roaring lion, walketh about, seeking whom he may devour."

The Apostle Peter was proclaimed to be a courageous and committed follower of Jesus, however when reality hit, Peter's fear for his life took control and Satan was the victor. The importance of prayer is paramount in our battle with the world and Satan's demons. As Peter we are weak with many frailties and we need God's strength to carry us through the many challenges we face on a daily basis.

Mark 14:54 reads, "And Peter followed him afar off, even into the palace of the high priest: and sat with the servants, and warmed himself at the fire."

As believers we have both successes and failures as we go through many experiences throughout our lives. We cannot be bystanders warming ourselves by the fire as Peter. We as believers are commissioned to follow God's plan for our lives.

Luke 22:31–32 reads, "And the Lord said, Simon, Simon, behold, Satan hath desired to have you, that he may sift you as wheat. But I have prayed for thee, that thy faith fail not: and when thou art converted, strengthen thy breather."

Jesus reminded Peter that Satan would like to destroy him and throw his ashes to the wind. Jesus also told Peter that he had prayed for him that his faith would be strong and he would continue to lead the Apostles.

Luke 22:61–62 reads, "And the Lord turned, and looked upon Peter. And Peter remembered the word of the Lord, how he had said unto him, Before the cock crow, thou shalt deny me thrice. And Peter went out, and wept bitterly."

The Apostle Peter had failed miserably and he felt the entire weight of his sin as Jesus looked straight into his soul. Surely Peter must have felt his life had ended and he was of no value to any person. Satan had used fear to bring Peter to his knees in unimaginable sorrow.

God understands our frailties and shows His mercy and grace to us as He did with the Apostle Peter. Peter had spent three years with Jesus and had witnessed countless miracles and blessings. Peter had committed himself to following Jesus and was willing to defend Jesus at all costs. However, the Apostle Peter had to experience the unbelievable sorrow from his denial to understand and develop the strength to confront the issues that he was going to encounter in the rest of his ministry. Our Lord and Savior with great love and mercy will allow challenges in our lives that we may grow in strength and share that love and strength with others.

1 Peter 4:12–14 reads, "Beloved, think it not strange concerning the fiery trial which is to try you, as though some strange thing happened unto you. But rejoice, inasmuch as ye are partakers of Christ's sufferings; that, when his glory shall be revealed, ye may be glad also with exceeding joy. If ye be reproached for the name of Christ, happy are ye; for the spirit of glory and of God resteth upon you: on their part he is evil spoken of, but on your part he is glorified."

The trials we experience throughout our life are extremely valuable in molding our character and allowing us to relate to others going through those same experiences. The pain, the joy, and emotions that fill our life are an integral part of our spirit that gives us the sensitivity to appreciate and understand what others are feeling and thinking. The Holy Spirit will direct you to those people in need and will give you the words to say and in some cases tell you what part you need to accomplish.

1 John 1:8–9 reads, "If we say that we have no sin, we deceive ourselves, and the truth is not in us. If we confess our sins, he is faithful and just to forgive us our sins, and to cleanse us from all unrighteousness."

Application

As believers we are still natural man or fallen man. We still sin and in many cases we sin without our realizing it because of our limited understanding of God's purpose in our lives. All of man's hearts are desperately evil and have problems understanding the spiritual aspect of his life. As believers we are new creatures and the Holy Spirit now directs us and submits our prayers for God's blessings and strength. As believers we recognize sin and develop a sensitivity to sin and ask for forgiveness when we fail. We are still in a daily battle with Satan and his demons, and need to be in prayer asking for God's strength and wisdom in dealing with sin.

Ephesians 1:11–13 reads, "In whom also we have obtained an inheritance, being predestinated according to the purpose of him who worketh all things after the counsel of his own will: That we should be to the praise of his glory, who first trusted in Christ. In whom ye also trusted, after that ye heard the word of truth, the gospel of your salvation: in whom also after that ye believed, ye were sealed with that Holy Spirit of promise."

As believers we are sealed with the Holy Spirit and have the inheritance of eternal life. The Holy Spirit is the believers' advocate, protector, encourager, and acts as a guarantee of the inheritance for salvation. A believer with the assistance of the Holy Spirit continues the battle each day with sin. However, the Holy Spirit provides the believer with a greater sensitivity to sin and allows the believer the knowledge to avoid sin.

The Apostle John and the other Apostles matured greatly during the three years of ministry with Jesus and continued that maturity during their entire life. The Apostle John lost self control when he asked Jesus to burn a Samaritan village to the ground for not welcoming Jesus on his travels through the village. Jesus rebuked the disciples and said he came to save man and not destroy man.

Luke 9:54–55 reads, "And when his disciples James and John saw this, they said, Lord, wilt thou that we command fire to come down from heaven, and consume them, even as Elijah did? But he turned, and rebuked them, and said, Ye know not what manner of spirit ye are of. For the Son of man is not come to destroy man's lives, but to save them. And they went to another village."

James and John (Sons of Thunder) were brothers who both became extremely angry and lost control of their emotions and wanted God to bring down fire from the heavens to destroy this Samaritan village.

Proverbs 14:29 reads, "He that is slow to wrath is of great understanding: but he that is hasty of spirit exalteth folly."

A person that is impatient and loses control of their temper will suffer the consequences in some way. As believers we struggle daily against principalities, against powers, and against wickedness. One of Satan's and his demon's priorities is to prevent you from accomplishing God's will for your life. God has a plan for your life and Satan will do everything he can do to prevent you from fulfilling that plan. If you find yourself consumed by anger you need take time before you respond and do or say something that you will later regret. It is important that we do not get distracted from God's plan for our lives and return to God's will as soon as possible.

The Apostle John spoke of self control and the importance of not loving the things of the world. An idol is anything that consumes our time and energy and takes the place of God. Idols can be the love of possessions, money, recognition, and many more things that hold a greater value or a priority than the worship of God. A non-believer is enslaved to sin and the worship of idols, Satan and his demons. A person who is a believer has the Holy Spirit living in their life and has broken Satan's shackles.

1 John 2:15–17 reads, "Love not the world, neither the things that are in the world. If any man love the world, the love of the father is not in him. For all that is in the world, the lust of the flesh, and the lust of the eyes, and the pride of life, is not of the Father, but is of the world. And the world passeth away, and the lust thereof: but he that doeth the will of God abideth for ever."

A person who loves Jesus Christ and follows God's commandments will break free of the sins of the world, its' idols and commune with the Holy Spirit. The Holy Spirit allows the believer to take control of his life and start to live a life that is focused on pleasing God and spending his time and energy helping others.

Psalm 119:11–16 reads, "Thy word have I hid in mine heart, that I might not sin against thee. Blessed art thou, O Lord: teach me thy statutes. With my lips have I declared all the judgments of thy mouth. I have rejoiced in the way of thy testimonies, as much as in all riches. I will meditate in thy precepts, and have respect unto thy ways. I will delight myself in thy statutes: I will not forget thy word."

The believer is able to take on greater understanding and appreciation of God's word as he spends more time in meditation.

11.

Conclusion

GOD SELECTED MOSES, ELIJAH, James, Peter, and John as witnesses to the Transfiguration because they represented major transformations in God's plan for mankind. These witnesses represented important periods in time in God's plan for all of mankind that elapsed from the Old to the New Testament. These men witnessed Jesus' glorified deity and thereby bearing witness to Jesus as the one Almighty God and Savior and Lord for all of mankind. These men were selected not because of their status in society or because of their talents; they were selected because of their heart, spirit and soul. They were men that had many character flaws and frailties as do most people. They failed many times and gave many excuses for not fulfilling God's plan.

God is able to look into the heart of a person and determine if that person will grow in faith and be obedient to God's word. They were all men that grew in great humility and would all fall at God's feet in worship. God looked at these men not for who they were, but for what they would become.

1 Samuel 16:7 reads, "But the Lord said unto Samuel, Look not on his countenance, or on the height of the stature; because I have refused him: for the Lord seeth not as man seeth; for man looketh on the outward appearance, but the Lord looketh on the heart."

God's Spirit indwelled these men and communed with their hearts and souls. From the beginning of creation the Holy Spirit has been actively comforting, convicting, and blessing those that have been anointed by faith.

Genesis 1:2 reads, "And the earth was without form, and void: and darkness was upon the face of the deep. And the Spirit of God moved upon the face of the waters."

God created this glorious and wonderful earth for us to care for and enjoy. He also created men and women that they may experience God's blessings and grow in appreciation of all what life has to offer.

God is a loving God that wants all people to spend eternity with Him and to experience all of His grace, mercy, and blessings. However, to experience God's grace, mercy, and blessings for eternity one must place God first in their life and place all of their trust and faith in Him. The believers that have crossed over or will cross over the bridge built from the death of God's only Son, Jesus Christ will experience blessings too numerous to count and will be able to rejoice as they never have rejoiced before.

God's plan for mankind started at the beginning. The unfolding of God's plan involved God selecting men that would carry great responsibility at specific points in time. Life is a precious gift from God that is for all of mankind. This life is short and fragile and can be shortened further by disease, accidents, and any number of other circumstances. At first glance, it is difficult to understand why millions of people refuse to believe in Jesus and His message of salvation. Unfortunately, some of the reason for this refusal is related to many Christians that are only Christians on Sunday. This hypocrisy is seen by the common man and either delays or prevents any further consideration for making a decision to investigate Christianity. Another obstacle for making a decision to accept Christ is the heart of the common man and his love of sin. He or she may love and worship any number of pagan gods. As discussed early, man worships the same pagan gods as he did during the time of Elijah and Moses. The names may have changed from Baal to wealth, or Asherah to pleasure, but the idea has remained the same. Anything that stands between you and God or prevents you from worshiping God is a sin. Millions of people are not Christians and many have no desire to become a Christian. The result will be that only believers will be able to share eternity with their Creator.

The Transfiguration also reflects the Old Testament prophesies for the cross, resurrection, and God's saving grace. The Israelites were the descendants of Abraham and were to receive the blessings from God's promise to Abraham.

Genesis 12:1–3 reads, "Now the Lord had said unto Abram, get thee out of thy country, and from thy kindred, and from thy father's house, unto

Conclusion

a land that I will show thee. And I will make of thee a great nation, and I will bless thee, and make thy name great; and thou shalt be a blessing. And I will bless them that bless thee: and to thee shall all families of the earth be blessed."

At this point in time God makes a promise (Covenant) to Abraham that He will make Israel a great nation. That Covenant to make Israel great was also renewed to Abraham's descendants. God later confirmed the covenant with Abraham's son Isaac, Isaac's son Jacob, and Jacob's son Levi, Levi's son Kohath, Kohath's son Amram, and Amram's son Moses.

God transformed Moses into one of the worlds' greatest leaders and laid on him great responsibilities. Moses' life started as a baby adopted by the Pharaohs' daughter and was denied nothing during his childhood. He was given the best education but was conflicted about his place in life. Moses loved the Israelites and killed one of the Pharaoh's guards at the age of 40 and fled for his life. He spent the next 40 years in the wildness herding sheep and hiding from the Egyptian rule.

God took a sheep herder with many weaknesses and no confidence living in fear and changed him into a man with tremendous courage that would stand in front of the Pharaoh and demand that he release the Israelites from bondage.

Numbers 12:3 reads, "Now the man Moses was very meek, above all the men which were upon the face of the earth."

Psalm 103:7 reads, "He made know his ways unto Moses, his acts unto the children of Israel."

Moses was not only meek he was the meekest of all men. God needed a man that He could use and mold into a great leader and be obedient to His commandments. All believers will experience God's mercy as he develops in each man faith and humility. We all struggle with the natural man and his love of self. We are all on a journey that requires of us to grow in faith, obedience and in humility as we pray and open God's word and fill our souls with His love, mercy, and His direction. We are all like Moses in that we struggle with life and are not always open to God's direction.

Moses was transformed to God's man. Moses was the man that God wanted to lead the Israelites out of Egypt and out from under slavery.

Deuteronomy 34:10-12 reads, "And there arose not a prophet since in Israel like unto Moses, whom the Lord knew face to face. In all the signs and the wonders, which the Lord sent him to do in the land of Egypt to Pharaoh, and to all his servants, and to all his land. And in all that mighty

Witnesses to a Great Miracle

hand and in all the great terror which Moses showed in the sight of all Israel."

God transformed Moses to be the man to mark a new beginning and to fulfill the promise to Abraham to make Israel a great nation.

Elijah was a "Tishbite". A Hebrew name meaning "My God is Yahweh". As Moses, Elijah spent a great deal of the time in the wilderness surviving off the land. Elijah was a little known priest and prophet that managed to survive by living in caves with nothing other than the clothes on his back.

However, Elijah was a prophet of God and was very bold and courageous as he challenged the people to decide between God and Baal. Elijah prophesied that there would be three years of severe drought that would cause catastrophic harm to the country and its people.

God spoke through Elijah at a critical point in time. The people of Israel in the Northern Kingdom under King Ahab and Queen Jezebel were being forced to worship Baal and the other pagan gods. Queen Jezebel was a devote follower of the pagan gods and demanded that all the people worship these gods of stone. To resist or disobey this command could be met with death or severe punishment.

Elijah was a faithful prophet of God and a man that was completely dependent on God for direction and his daily needs. Elijah was not only obedient to God's direction, but he acted without fear as he approached King Ahab and demanded that he allow the people to worship the true God. As Moses, Elijah was a man that God talked to directly and indwelled his entire being. Both Moses and Elijah had many frailties and failed on many occasions.

1Kings 18:1 reads, "And it came to pass after many days, that the word of the Lord came to Elijah in the third year, saying, Go show thyself unto Ahab, and I will send rain upon the earth."

However, God was able to use these men because of their humble spirits and souls and their obedience to God's word regardless of the dangers. Both of these men with God's strength were able to face evil and ruthless rulers without being executed and make demands sighting God's commands.

The Apostle James, another one of God's witnesses to the Transfiguration, is recognized as the first Apostle to be martyred for his belief in the gospel. It is a point in time that marks the beginning when many of the Apostles would be martyred for their faith and their willingness to preach the word of God regardless of the consequences. The Apostle James' death

Conclusion

and martyrdom is a reflection of Jesus Christ's Crucifixion and the challenge that Jesus gave to James and John when they agreed to drink from His cup.

Mark 10:37-38 reads, "They said unto him, Grant unto us that we may sit, one on the right hand, and the other on thy left hand, in thy glory. But Jesus said unto them, ye know not what ye ask: can ye drink of the cup that I drink of and be baptized with that baptism that I am baptized with."

We are all natural men with limited understanding of God's love, mercy, glory, and plans. We have no concept of the sorrow and suffering that Jesus Christ had to endure from the wrath of God for sins of all mankind. We think and apply our own understanding, desires, and wishes to God's plan for all of mankind. We ask for things as natural man that are selfish and are not in keeping with God's spiritual plan for our life.

The Apostle James was one of the first and oldest of the Apostles and in some ways the most mature. When Jesus asked James (the greater) to follow him he did not hesitate to say yes. He was bold in his speaking and fearless in his approach to witnessing for the life and death of Jesus Christ his Savior. Jesus the Christ came into this world as a humble servant and as a man who revealed His love by healing thousands and explaining the way of salvation.

Isaiah 53:3-6 reads, "He is despised and rejected of men; a man of sorrows, and acquainted with grief: and we hid as it were our faces from him: he was despised, and we esteemed him not. Surely he hath borne our griefs, and carried our sorrows: yet we did esteem him stricken, smitten of God, and afflicted. But he was wounded for our transgressions, he was bruised for our iniquities: the chastisement of our peace was upon him; and with his stripes we are healed. All we like sheep have gone astray; we have turned every one to his own way; and the Lord hath laid on him the iniquity of us all."

Jesus came to this earth and lived his life as a humble servant as our example as to how to love our neighbor. As Moses and Elijah, James was a humble man of God. The Apostle James (the greater) was courageous and continued to preach fiery sermons (son of thunder) knowing the temple priests were plotting his demise. Eventually, King Herod arrested him and killed him with sword to the pleasure of the people. It is believed that the Apostle James approached his death singing the glories of his Savior.

The Apostle Peter was a very humble man and sensitive to those around him.

Luke 5:8 reads, "When Simon Peter saw it, he fell down at Jesus' knees, saying, Depart from me; for I am a sinful man, O Lord."

The Apostle Peter quickly realized that he was in the presence of God and that his life was full of sin. Peter's heart and soul was aware of God's presence and he had to humble himself at Jesus' feet to show respect and to plea for mercy. It was Peter who first recognized Jesus as His Savior and Lord.

Mathew 16:16 reads, "And Simon Peter answered and said, Thou art the Christ, the Son of the living God."

As Peter, we need to respect and humble ourselves in the presences of our Lord and Savior, Jesus the Christ, the Son of God.

Mathew 16:17-18 reads, "And Jesus answered and said unto him, Blessed art thou, Simon Bar-jona: for flesh and blood hath not revealed it unto thee, but my Father which is in heaven. And I say also thee, That thou art Peter and upon this rock I will build my church: and the gates of hell shall not prevail against it."

At this point in time we see another part of God's plan unfold for mankind as God tells Peter he will use him as a foundation for building His Church. This is obviously a great honor and an unspeakable privilege and a great responsibility for the Apostle Peter.

The Apostle Peter was a common man that made many mistakes, but God was patient and corrected him in love many times. From God's patient loving care the Apostle Peter grew in wisdom and understanding of what was required to be a servant.

Luke 5:10 reads, "And so was also James, and John, the sons of Zebedee, which were partners with Simon. And Jesus said unto Simon, Fear not; from henceforth thou shalt catch men."

The Apostles James, John, and Peter were all summoned by Jesus to be fishers of men. They were all in God's presence and they were all going to be trained by Jesus (the Son of God) to be servants to God's word.

The Apostle John was the youngest of the early Apostles and was the only Apostle that died of natural causes. The Apostle John was called by Jesus as the beloved disciple and was at present at most of the miracles.

John 21:20-22 reads, "Then Peter, turning about, seeth the disciple whom Jesus loved following; which also leaned on his breast at supper, and said, Lord, which is he that betrayeth thee? Peter seeing him saith to Jesus, Lord, and what shall this man do? Jesus saith unto him, If I will that he tarry till I come what is that to thee? Follow thou me."

Conclusion

Jesus refused to tell the Apostle Peter God's plan for the Apostle John's life. God's plan for the Apostle John was not known to any man. No man knows God's plan for any man. God's plan for each individual varies as different as each man's character.

The Apostle John learned from Jesus and grew to be a servant who was willing to suffer and sacrifice all for the gospel. He understood that humility was paramount if he was going to achieve any success in building the church through God. The Apostle John patiently suffered at Patmos where he lived in a cave for years.

The Apostle John was also passionate in his proclamation of the gospel and willingness to defend the truth. John also learned from Jesus his strong love for others and grew in humility as the church was blessed and grew. The Apostle John understood the importance of humility and to guard against the constant threat of self and pride. His passion for the truth and his compassion to be a servant was always paramount.

The witnesses to the Transfiguration (Moses, Elijah, James, Peter, and John) were men that God used to unfold his plan for all of mankind. Moses was used to fulfill God's promise to bring his people to the Promised Land. God used Elijah to turn his people from worshiping pagan gods to worshiping the one true God. James marked the beginning of the martyrdom of the Apostles. Peter's life laid the foundation for the purpose of building the church. John's long loving life was to identify the church as a loving extension of Jesus Christ for all of mankind. These witnesses of the Transfiguration represented God's plan for all of mankind, from the promise made to Abraham of a Promised Land to the book of Revelations written by the Apostle John.

John 1:14 reads, "And the Word was made flesh, and dwelt among us, and we beheld his glory, the glory as of the only begotten of the father, full of grace and truth."

The Transfiguration revealed the glory of Jesus and that He fulfilled and obeyed God's commands.

Mark 9:2–7 reads, "And after six days Jesus taketh with him Peter, and James and John, and leadeth them up into a high mountain apart by themselves: and he was transfigured before them. And his raiment became shining, exceeding white as snow; so as no fuller on earth can white them. And there appeared unto them Elijah with Moses: and they were talking with Jesus. And Peter answered and said to Jesus, Master, it is good for us to be here: and let us make three tabernacles; one for thee, and one for Mosses, and one for Elijah. For he wist not what to say; for they were sore afraid. And there was a cloud that overshadowed them: and voice came out of the cloud, saying, This is my beloved Son: hear him."

The Apostles Peter, James, and John were witnesses to the Transfiguration because they were allowed to be part of God's plan for mankind. They were also allowed to witness the Transfiguration to receive the blessing of seeing Jesus as he was transformed from a normal man to his form as a deity. This experience would have been seared into their memory and would have been a driving force for their entire life as they faced many challenges.

All these men (Moses, Elijah, James, Peter, and John) were all common men with many weakness, frailties, and failures. However, they were obedient to God's word, courageous with God's strength, and assumed great responsibilities in God's plan. They all understood that they were servants and were required to deliver God's message of love and salvation to all of mankind.

Luke 9:46–48 reads, "Then there arose a reasoning among them, which of them should be greatest. And Jesus, perceiving the thought of their heart, took a child, and set him by him. And said unto them, whoever, shall receive this child in my name receiveth me: and whosoever shall receive me receiveth him that sent me: for he that is least among you all, the same shall be great."

Jesus Christ came to this earth not as a king but as a servant to save those that were lost in their sin. Following Jesus and obeying God's commands requires one to be a servant to others. Moses, Elijah, James, Peter, and John were servants to all of mankind and understood they were servants to all of those they lead by following God's direction in mercy, grace, and love. They were all common men that learned to be humble servants that patiently waited on God for direction.

As believers we are transformed from being a self-centered individual to a person that places Jesus Christ as our center. We grow in maturity as we become more obedient and are challenged to accept more responsibilities. Our relationship with God evolves as he sees we are trustworthy and able to accomplish spiritual tasks.

The transformation of a believer is a lifelong process of living as a servant to others with the strength of the Holy Spirit.

Romans 12:1–3 reads, "I beseech you therefore, brethren, by the mercies of God, that ye present your bodies a living sacrifice, holy, acceptable unto God, which is your reasonable service. And be not conformed to this

Conclusion

world: but be ye transformed by the renewing of your mind, that ye may prove what is that good, and acceptable, and perfect, will of God. For I say, through the grace given unto you, to every man that is among you, not to think of himself more highly then he ought to think; but to think soberly, according as God hath dealt to every man the measure of faith."

As believes we are in a process of transforming our lives from one of being self-centered and living as a natural man to one of surrendering and submitting our life to serving others. Moses, Elijah, James, Peter, and John were men that lived each day as servants following God's direction. Moses was a humble servant of God who led the Israelites to the Promised Land. Elijah was the humble servant that God used to destroy the worship of pagan gods and return Israel to the worship of the one true God. James was the humble servant who gave his life for furtherance of the gospel. Peter was the humble servant that God used as a foundation for the church. John was the humble servant that was used by God to build the church and deliver God's word. Their wisdom, courage, strength, obedience, and loving kindness were a reflection of God in their lives and His plan for all of mankind. God the Almighty loving mercy, grace, faithfulness, and patience are available to all of mankind.

God sent His only Son to become a man, a humble servant, and to be obedient to His word even unto death on the cross.

Philippians 2:8–11 reads, "And being found in fashion as a man, he humbled himself, and became obedient unto death, even death on the cross. Wherefore God also hath highly exalted him, and given him a name which is above every name. That at the name of Jesus every knee should bow, of things in heaven, and things in earth, and things under the earth; And that every tongue should confess that Jesus Christ is Lord, to the glory of God the Father."

We have been given example after example of how to live as a humble servant. As believers we are being transformed from the natural man to the spiritual man. This lifelong process will end as we are all transfigured into another form as our faces begin to shine brightly, as our lives begin to become more like our Savior and Lord, and as we begin to sing praises to our Creator.

Notes

REFERENCES THROUGHOUT THE BOOK are from the King James translation of the Holy Bible.

Spurgeon, Charles H. *Spurgeon's Sermon Notes: Over 250 Sermons including Notes, Commentary and Illustrations*, David Otis Fuller, ed. Grand Rapids, Mt Kregel, 1990.

Buswell, James Oliver Jr. *Problems in the Prayer Life: From a Pastor's Question Box.* Chicago: The Bible Institute, 1928.

Geikie, Cunningham. *The life and Words of Christ.* New York: Appleton and Company. 1879.

Brenton, Lancelot C. *The Septuagint with Apocrypha: Greek and English.* Hendrickson, 1986

Bruce, Alexander Balmain. *Training of the Twelve.* Keats Publishing, Inc., 1979

Webster, Douglas D. *Finding Spiritual Direction.* InterVarsity Press, 1991

Lewis, C.S., *Miracles*, Harper One, 2000

Edersheim, Rev. D., *Sketches of Jewish Social Life in the Day of Christ.* Hodder & Stoughton, 1989.

www.ingramcontent.com/pod-product-compliance
Lightning Source LLC
Chambersburg PA
CBHW071438160426
43195CB00013B/1957